CLIMB EVERY
MOUNTAIN

The Life Story of Wales H. Madden, Jr. as told to Jon Mark Beilue

JON MARK BEILUE

authorHOUSE®

AuthorHouse™
1663 Liberty Drive
Bloomington, IN 47403
www.authorhouse.com
Phone: 1 (800) 839-8640

Published by AuthorHouse 12/01/2016

ISBN: 978-1-5246-5008-7 (sc)
ISBN: 978-1-5246-5006-3 (hc)
ISBN: 978-1-5246-5007-0 (e)

Library of Congress Control Number: 2016919019

CONTENTS

For my family and friends.
See ya down the road,
Wales H. Madden, Jr.

FOREWORD

The first time I knew of Wales Madden had to be sometime in the 1980s. I was then a sportswriter at the *Amarillo Globe-News* and had a desk right in front of renowned sports columnist Putt Powell, who had been working at the newspaper since the 1930s. On occasion Putt would reference Wales in his columns if the subject matter were the Texas Longhorns. On this day, he called Wales.

Putt had a long streak of covering consecutive Texas-Oklahoma football games, but a new sports information director for Texas called to tell Putt that his media credential request was denied, that only regular beat writers of the two teams or newspapers with a certain circulation size could be accommodated. Putt protested a little bit but then hung up and quickly dialed another number.

"Wales, this is Putt," I could hear him say over my shoulder. "Wonder if you could give me a little help..."

Putt explained the situation, and he and Wales had some small talk before the call ended. In no more than five minutes, Putt's phone rang again. It was the UT sports information director. Putt had his press credential, and I, a young kid in my twenties, was awfully impressed.

In just a few minutes, it spoke to Wales Madden's influence and his willingness to help a friend. How symbolic. Wales has been using his influence to help others all his life.

To say that I've been a longtime friend of Wales Madden, Jr., would not be accurate. Our paths crossed for the first time five or six years ago. I wrote a couple of columns-one on his being honored by the local University of Texas Exes chapter and another on his pride and joy, the Harrington Fellows.

He would occasionally call me to compliment something I had written or suggest an idea for a future column topic. In 2012, he tearfully called to tell me-in effect, alerting the *Globe-News*-that his beloved wife Abbie, of nearly sixty years, had died. I wrote the obituary on Abbie Cowden Madden.

But to say we were close friends would have been overstating things. I hope that's no longer the case, not after 2016.

In September 2015, Wales called with a suggestion. Would I write a biography of his life? Wow, how old are you again, Wales? That's a lot of life. What all have you done again? Wow, what have you *not* done?

To be honest, I didn't know if I had the time to commit to such a project. I kind of put it off. Perhaps Wales would forget or find a better writer to tell his life story, but he called again in December 2015 with the same proposal. This time I knew I had to make it happen. My goodness, I reasoned, if he's asking me again, he's run out of people to ask. It's either me or nothing, and Wales deserves to have his incredible life in print for posterity.

So we came up with a workable plan. After the holidays, beginning in January 2016, I would meet with him weekly. Fridays were generally the slowest of the workdays for me, so we set up meetings in his Amarillo Building office at 11 a.m. each Friday.

When I told a friend of mine what I was doing and how I was going about it, he said, "'Tuesdays with Morrie,' 'Fridays with Wales.' It just might work."

I'd like to think it did. We met seventeen different Fridays, usually for about an hour and a half. Often, his close friend Virginia Maynard and/or son Wales III and daughter-in-law Nita would sit in. Usually, it was just to listen, but sometimes it was to help the conversation along.

It was then those long ago newspaper clippings and awards came to life. It wasn't long until these times confirmed what I suspected-if a Mt. Rushmore were made of Amarillo giants, someone better start chiseling Wales' features.

His Amarillo High days. Navy service in World War II. His time of leadership at the University of Texas and UT Law School. His marriage and family, early work with Shamrock, and a work partnership and friendship forged with Boone Pickens.

There was a lifelong dedication of service to his beloved alma mater, UT, where he held just about any office worth holding, including a member of the board of regents. There was his work for political causes and candidates and his tireless efforts on behalf of his hometown, from philanthropic causes to fundraising behind the scenes. In 1971, he was the *Globe-News* Man of the Year, but he could have been man of the year most any year.

Oh, how could I forget his love of the great outdoors and the pure pleasure of hiking up another trail or fishing for trout in a clear cold stream?

He was a friend to three presidents, several governors, and a billionaire, but also a friend to those without much means. Our conversations were peppered with, "He's a really good friend of mine," or, "He was a great guy."

Only once did he say, "He was a real son-of-a-bitch." I'll leave unsaid who that might be. If you know Wales, you might know who it was. If you don't, you wouldn't know who he was talking about anyway. All I know is if Wales, who rarely met a stranger, said he was an SOB, he must really have been.

Through his nearly ninety years, this much became clear to me: Wales Madden loves people. He loves his God and family first and foremost, but he has a real affinity for his fellow man, and so much of his decades of service, of not being able to say no, of his self-deprecating personality and sense of humor, was because he loved people and loved doing for others.

From helping a fellow friend and sportswriter to projects that made a lasting difference on hundreds of lives, that's Wales Madden's legacy. That's a life well-lived, and in some small way, I hope our Fridays with each other convey that.

Jon Mark Beilue
Columnist
Amarillo Globe-News

ACKNOWLEDGEMENTS

Photos and scans:

Bill Hughes

Daily Texan

Amarillo Globe-News

The Cowden and Madden Family albums

The White House and other political staff photographers

Various photographers and studios that are no longer with us

Editing:

Margaret Aycock

Nita and Wales Madden III

WALES H. MADDEN, JR.

Biographical Data

Personal

Born September 1, 1927, Amarillo, Texas

Father:	Wales H. Madden, Amarillo attorney (deceased). A Harvard graduate, he was actively involved in the legal practice and in the community. He served as Regional Chairman of the War Labor Board in World War II.
Mother:	Kathryn Nash Madden (deceased)
Grandfather:	S. H. Madden (deceased) He was the first District Attorney in Potter County and in the 1880s successfully negotiated with Santa Fe Railway in Chicago to bring its line through Amarillo destined for the West Coast.

Attended Amarillo public schools

Graduated Amarillo High School with honors, 1945

Joined Navy March, 1945 and served until August, 1946. Duty in the Pacific aboard the USS *Lipan* ATF 85.

Attended The University of Texas: BA-1950, LLB-1952

Married Alma Faye Cowden ("Abbie") daughter of Clyde & Jessie Cowden, Midland, Texas in 1952. Abbie passed away August 26, 2012.

Daughter:	Straughn Madden Macfarlan, married	
	Two children:	Mac, Callie
	Husband:	Dean
Son:	Wales H. Madden III, married	
	Two children:	Wales IV, Hamilton
	Wife:	Nita

1955 Elder, First Presbyterian Church of Amarillo. At that time, he was youngest elder on record.

Professional & Business

Attorney, The Shamrock Oil and Gas Corporation, 1952-60

Partner, Selecman and Madden, 1965-85

Private Practice, 1985-present, albeit mostly retired

Member, Board of Directors, First National Bank of Amarillo, 1961-1993

Member, Board of Directors, Boatman's First National Bank, 1993-1996

Reorganized after merger, then First National Bank, 1997-2002

Wells Fargo Advisory Board, 2002-2007

Mesa Petroleum Board, including predecessor board, 1967-1996

Professional Activities

President, Amarillo Area Bar Association, 1957

President, Junior State Bar of Texas, 1957

Member, American Bar Association

Member, Fellows of American Bar Foundation

Texas Bar Foundation, Life Fellow

Chairman, Senator Phil Gramm's Federal Judiciary Evaluation Committee, 1985-93

Chairman, Senators Phil Gramm and Kay Bailey Hutchison's Federal Judicial Advisory Group, 1995-2001

Member Senators Phil Gramm and Kay Bailey Hutchison's Federal Judiciary Evaluation Committee, 2001-2011
The genius of this Committee was Senator Gramm's determination to find qualified, conservative, honest people to accept appointment to the Federal Bench and to abrogate political patronage. It worked. No other state adheres to this "Open Door" policy.

Educational Interests

Member, The University of Texas Committee of 75, 1957-1960

Member, Board of Regents, Amarillo College, 1958-59

Member, Board of Trustees, Trinity University, San Antonio, 1962-93

Member, Board of Regents, The University of Texas System, 1959-65, appointed by Governor Price Daniel

Member, Board of Trustees, The University of Texas Law School Foundation, 1967-present

Member, Men's Athletics Council, The University of Texas, 1974-81

Member, Development Board, The University of Texas, 1965-present (Chairman 1985-87)

President, The Ex-Students' Association, The University of Texas, 1975 and 1976, current member

Member, The Littlefield Society, The University of Texas, 1990-present

Member, The Chancellor's Council, The University of Texas, inception-present (Chairman 1998-99)

Member, Legislative Committee on Faculty Compensation in State Universities and Colleges, 1965-69, appointed by Speaker Ben Barnes. Recommendations led to legislative authorization of faculty leaves for the first time; the creation of the Optional Retirement Program for Higher Education, previously not available; and the provision of health and life insurance for faculties.

Member, Governor's Committee on Public School Education, 1966-69, appointed by Governor John Connally

Member, Texas Higher Education Coordinating Board, 1969-73, appointed by Governor John Connally

Member, Legislative Committee on State/Local Relationships in Financing the Minimum Foundation School Program, 1969-71, appointed by Lt. Governor Ben Barnes

Chairman, The University of Texas Centennial Commission, 1980-84, appointed by Board of Regents.

Member, Select Committee on Higher Education, 1985-87, appointed by Lt. Governor Bill Hobby

Chairman, Dallas Regional Selection Panel, President's Commission on White House Fellowships, 1989-90

Member, Texas Higher Education Coordinating Board Committee on Statewide Governance of Higher Education, 1990

Chairman, Board for International Food and Agricultural Development and Economic Cooperation, 1990-94, appointed by President George H. W. Bush. First person to serve as Chairman who was not a president of a university.

Chairman, William Livingston Fellowship Endowments, The University of Texas, 1994

Member, Governing Board, Amarillo National Resource Center, 1995-2002

Board Member, The University of Texas Donald D. Harrington Fellows Program, 2000-present. This program operates through The University of Texas at Austin and has become internationally renowned for its contribution to higher education worldwide.

Member, Commission of 125, The University of Texas, 2002

Awards and Activities

Amarillo Young Man of the Year, 1959

Amarillo Man of the Year, 1971

Amarillo High School Hall of Fame, 1976

Outstanding Alumnus Award, Tom Clark Chapter of Phi Alpha Delta, The University of Texas Law School, 1959

International Alumnus of the Year, Phi Delta Theta, 1971

Distinguished Alumnus Award, The University of Texas, 1979

Outstanding Alumnus Award, The University of Texas Law School, 1986

1992 Presidential Citation, The University of Texas at Austin

Santa Rita Award, The University of Texas at Austin, 2002, selected by Board of Regents

Outstanding Fifty-Year Lawyer Award, Texas Bar Foundation, 2003. No more than six recipients are selected each year.

Listed in Who's Who in America

Listed in Who's Who in American Education

Mirabeau B. Lamar Award for Outstanding Leadership in Higher Education, 1984

First President, Texas Panhandle Heritage Foundation, 1960-62. Chairman of the drive to fund building the amphitheatre in the Palo Duro Canyon and to produce *Texas!* Current board member

Member of Partners in Palo Duro Canyon Foundation, Volunteer Guide

One of the individuals Interviewed by UT Oral History Project of The University of Texas during 2006.

Interviewed in 2009 by *The Alcalde* for 125 years of the Texas Exes.

President, Amarillo Chamber of Commerce, 1963

President, Amarillo Area Foundation, 1979

Co-chairman, Amarillo Strategic Area Plan, 1987-88

Member, Board of Directors, Cal Farley's Boys Ranch, 1967-1985. Current honorary member

Member, Board of Directors, The Don and Sybil Harrington Foundation, 1982-present, President 1988-90

Member, Board of Directors, The Don and Sybil Harrington Cancer Center, 1994-96

Co-chairman, Panhandle 2000, 1991-present

Member, Constitutional Revision Commission of Texas, 1973-74, appointed by Lt. Governor Bill Hobby

Member, Governor's Task Force on State Trust and Asset Management, 1982, appointed by Governor Bill Clements

Member, The Philosophical Society of Texas, 1984-present

Member, President's Export Council, 1980-85, appointed by President Ronald Reagan

Member, Citizens' Committee on Property Tax Relief, 1996, appointed by Governor George W. Bush

Member, Texas Water Development Board, 1998-2003, appointed by Governor George W. Bush
Chairman 2002-03, appointed by Governor Rick Perry

Co-chairman, Friends of the University of Texas System PAC, 1998-present

Recent Political Activities

State Co-chairman, Phil Gramm for U.S. Senate Campaign, 1984

State Chairman, Phil Gramm for U.S. Senate Campaign, 1990

State Vice Chairman, Bush for President Campaign, 1988

Chairman, Texas Region VIII, Victory '88

At-large Delegate, 1988 Republican National Convention

Envoy and representative of President George H.W. Bush at inauguration of Uruguayan President Lacalle, 1990

Member, National Finance Committee, Bush/Quayle '92

Member, National Steering Committee, Lawyers for Bush/Quayle '92

Member, Advisory Committee, Texas Victory '92

At-large Delegate, 1992 Republican National Convention

Member, Senator Kay Bailey Hutchison's Finance Campaign Executive Committee, 1996-2011

Member, Transition Team, Attorney General John Cornyn, 1998

State of Texas Co-chairman, Lawyers for Bush/Chaney 2000

National Finance Steering Committee, Bush/Chaney 2001-2009

Regional Co-chairman, Kay Bailey Hutchison for Governor 2009

College Activities

Enrolled at The University of Texas at Austin, September, 1946. BA-1950, LLB-1952

Member of the following:

Phi Delta Theta-Social Fraternity

Phi Eta Sigma-Freshman honorary (President)

Pi Sigma Alpha-Government honorary (President)

Phi Alpha Delta-Legal honorary

Cowboys-Foreman (President)

Friars-Abbot (President)

Interfraternity Council-President

Student Assistant, Government Department

First award for Most Outstanding Male Student, 1951

President of Student Body, 1951

Intramural sports-football (all intramural team), soccer, wrestling (intramural champion), water polo

Member, University wrestling team (club sport)

THE EARLY YEARS

Wales Madden, Jr.'s, grandfather S.H. Madden, moved to Texas from Tennessee. An attorney, Madden settled in Clarendon, one of the Texas Panhandle's earliest communities, where Wales' father, Wales H. Madden, Sr., was born in 1894.

The eldest of the Maddens longed to move to the growing town of Amarillo, sixty miles to the northwest. There being no railroad at the time, his family arrived by horse and buggy. Madden later negotiated with the Santa Fe Railway in Chicago to bring its line through Amarillo on the way to the West Coast, action that accelerated the city's growth. S.H. Madden became Potter County's first District Attorney, with his son and grandson each becoming lawyers as well.

S.H. Madden pre-1924

Wales Madden, Jr., was born in Amarillo on September 1, 1927, to parents Kathryn and Wales Madden, Sr. By that time his grandfather had died, and his father, a Harvard graduate, was a partner in the law firm of Adkins, Pipkin, Madden and Kefer in the Fisk Building.

Wales H. Madden Sr.

"My mother was sweet, very sensitive to people. She was very bright, almost withdrawn," Wales said. "My father was not outwardly loving of me, but I could sense how much he really did love me."

WM and Katy Madden about 1934

"There was something wrong with my parents' relationship. Not to say it was estrangement, but there was not a loving cordiality. You would come into a room sometimes, and they would quit talking. It was quiet. It was distant."

Wales was a boy during the Depression, born two years before the stock market crash of 1929. Even then, he sensed people were hurting and money was tight. His home was at 1017 W. Tenth Avenue, next door to his aunt, Minnis Hall. Tenth Avenue was a branch of Highway 66 which connected Chicago and Los Angeles. With cars churning east and west, Wales witnessed what he called "a total absence of comfort," which included children riding on the hoods. When passengers would spy the water hose at the Madden home, "They would stop and ask if they could get a drink of water and fill up their car with our hose," he said. "I was right out there helping fill those cars up. That was a big deal."

Although Wales Madden was only five years old in the early 1930s, he saw people for who they were, not who society thought they should be. The 1930s were still a time of segregation and Jim Crow laws that strictly defined black and white, yet Wales didn't see it that way. All he knew was that the black housekeeper, Beulah Wells, was the family maid and that he liked her. Her husband Chester worked for the Santa Fe Railroad, and they lived in a garage apartment at the Madden home on Tenth Avenue.

Beulah (aka Ninny)

Sometimes Beulah would take Wales with her to shop downtown. They would enter the Kress department store where the young lad would see evidence of segregation.

"I can almost smell that store," Wales said.

Inside, there were two water fountains, one marked "colored" and one marked "white." That seemed odd.

"We both were getting a drink, and I pulled her over to the one marked for whites," Wales said. "She said, 'I can't drink out of your fountain.' I'm sure it angered me more than startled me. I asked her if I could drink out of hers. She said, 'Yes,' and I remember thinking that this isn't fair. Why can't she drink out of this fountain? That branded me internally. I thought there was something unfair about this distinction between blacks and whites."

When Wales was about five or six years old, he very much liked to tag along with Beulah and Chester to an all-black church gathering in a tent on Amarillo's north side.

"I loved going," Wales said. "I liked to hear them sing and clap and to run up and down the aisle. I could smell the scent of the canvas tent. I would hop out of their arms and run down a dirt path to where the minister was preaching. At first, there was a lot of 'ooohh,' but they soon saw I was completely sincere about wanting to be up there singing and dancing, doing whatever they were doing."

"I was the only white there, sitting down, standing up or otherwise," he said. "That may not be totally true, but I can't recall seeing anyone with the color of skin that I had, but I didn't attach enough significance to really care what I was doing or who I was with. I was completely comfortable with the black congregation and black minister," Wales said. "I liked their singing and the fact those people were completely honest and open."

Wales' father was not much of a church-going man, but his mother Kathryn was a devout Catholic. When he was older, Wales accompanied his mother to St. Mary's Catholic Church, partly out of curiosity and partly to be with her.

"I really did not feel comfortable because I felt as I understood what was being said, some of it in Latin, the main purpose was not so much to let us feel at peace or in love with Christ, but to worry about those people who were not in that situation," Wales said.

Two of Wales' closest friends, Rudy and Bobby Bauman, also attended St. Mary's. As in Wales' family, their mother was strong in the Catholic faith, but their father was not.

"On Sundays, my mother would let me sit up in the balcony with Bobby and Rudy," he said. "One of the things they wanted was for people up there to sing. When Bobby, Rudy, and I got up there and started singing, they asked us to be quiet.

"I didn't know what the word 'hypocrite' was at that stage, but I felt like I didn't want to be there because I didn't believe in the sermons."

Wales never felt at home in the Catholic faith. When Latin was spoken, it was hard for a young boy to grasp what was occurring, and he felt ill at ease. Not so in the Negro church. The exuberance of the congregation, the emotional singing, the smiles and laughter stayed with Wales. As he grew older, he wanted a worship experience that was not rote and dry but was from the heart.

Those early events marked Wales, as it was his first real introduction to church. During his high school years, he was still struggling to find a place for the Lord in his life. He knew he felt something when in a church that he didn't feel anywhere else.

"Even recalling that now, I'm getting cold chills down my back," Wales said. "I didn't know what it was. I can honestly attribute it to the love of Christ because I don't really think I understood all of that."

His Christian faith would take hold during World War II and continue the rest of his life. He also would continue to be color blind, fraternizing with blacks in the Navy, which could be frowned upon, as well as later appointing blacks to positions on the student cabinet at the University of Texas.

Wales has never been without friends, including an imaginary one called "Don Don Pee Pee." In his early years he thought Barbara

Boxwell was the prettiest girl in the whole world. She spent time at his house playing and climbing a cherry tree.

Pat Oles was a lifelong friend, first as kids, later at the University of Texas, and then back in Amarillo where Oles was a longtime practicing physician. In the beginning, they just shared juvenile hijinks. He and Pat became what Wales called "a nuisance." At age ten, they had air rifles to shoot birds and car windows. He shot out the windows of a neighbor's car. Unfortunately, the neighbors were Rudy and Bobby Bauman. "That was a mistake," Wales said. They later returned with air rifles of their own, then it was the Bauman brothers against Wales and Pat.

Bill Hughes   Pat Oles   Rudy Bauman

Photo by B Hughes

These early enemies became fast friends through high school, particularly after Wales agreed to join the Baumans in a game of tackling people who happened to walk between two adjoining sidewalks.

When the Baumans moved to Twenty-fourth and Washington, vacant lots were all around. They used the land to build their own caves with roofs. Wales joined with the Baumans to defend their territory using rubber guns, often against the Atteburys who lived about ten blocks away.

"They were a bunch of bandits, and we didn't like each other," he said. "They attacked us, and we had to defend ourselves. Ultimately, we became friends and defended ourselves against other neighbors."

Wales befriended Bill Attebury, as tough and good a person as he would ever know. He saw how tough one day when their cave was attacked by outsiders.

"Bill and this other guy were wrasslin' around, and he took Bill down," Wales said. "He had Bill's arm pinned back behind his back saying, 'Give, give, give.' And Attebury said, 'Break the son of a bitch, I'm not giving.' "

Bottom to top: Rudy Bauman, WM, Pat Oles
Photo by B Hughes

However, it was Oles and Wales who were attached at the hip. Well, maybe not always. With Pat supposedly leading the way, they had an early go at vandalism. They ran up and down alleys turning over trash cans. One afternoon, Pat had a head start, and Wales, being a bit pudgy in those days, was trying to catch up. A woman had some clothes hanging on a clothesline on the north side of the alley. Pat pulled clothes off the line, which seemed like a good idea at the time.

"Getting over the fence was kinda hard, but getting back over when she came out with a broom was even harder," Wales said. "I was too fat, and Pat just left me there."

Wales ran down the alley, crossed Tenth Avenue, and figured he could hide somewhere. He jumped in the trash bin, the odor of which he can still smell seventy-five years later. He pulled the top over his head, thinking he was safe, until the top was lifted by an Amarillo policeman. The officer asked him who he was and then escorted him to his father. Wales, Sr., happened to be home.

"That was not good for me," Wales said, "and Oles didn't even get in trouble at all."

Nor did he when Oles had another not-so-brilliant idea. He lived next door to the Amarillo school superintendent, Mr. Rogers. They took his water hose, put it through the mailbox slot which ran into the house, and turned on the water.

"I don't remember what the consequence of that was," Wales said, "but he couldn't have been very happy."

Wales went to Wolflin Elementary School and Central Junior High, which was next to Amarillo High School, the city's only high school at the time. He was an average student in school, not really motivated to excel; however, that changed when he was a sophomore at Amarillo High. The teacher was Effie Burkhalter, a striking woman who manifested a profound presence in the hallways. The English teacher, who was also Wales' homeroom teacher, had a heart-to-heart discussion with the underachieving sophomore.

"I was not as capable as I could have been," Wales said. "She made me stay after school and said, 'You're wasting your education. You're much smarter than the grades you're making, and you ought to be ashamed of yourself.'

"I get all choked up thinking about Effie Burkhalter for pulling me aside and saying that I really ought to do better. It was a turning point. No one ever told me I could make better grades. It gave me a goal."

Wales buckled down in his classes, and his grades reached the level Effie Burkhalter knew he could attain. His favorite classes were the odd mixture of mechanical drawing and English.

By his own admission, Wales wasn't big enough or talented enough for the Sandie football team. Instead, he was a cheerleader. He was also on student council and, through smarts and personality, worked his way to being among the school's leaders.

1944 AHS Cheerleaders
Photo by Amarillo High School student staff

In addition to boyhood friends Pat Oles and the Bauman brothers, Wales became lifelong friends with soon-to-be star basketball player Boone Pickens as well as with Bill Hughes.

Elden Durrett, whom Wales called "easily the brightest guy I hung around with," Walter Kellogg, Eugene Lyons, and Pat Babb were all in his social circle. They thought nothing of being a nuisance at Lovers' Leap west of town. Hughes was the one who had a car, and as many as possible piled in.

"He could take care of it. He could fix it. He and I and four or five others went to Colorado several times in his car, literally sitting on the fenders," Wales said. "We had built a platform in the back end of it and would lie back there on a mattress. We didn't have to worry about suitcases because we didn't have any."

Keith James Rudy Bauman Eldon Durrett Pat Babb
Pat Oles Wales Madden Tony Martin Bill Hughes

WM driving and Rudy with "friends" in Bill Hughes car
Photos by B Hughes

For Wales and all his friends there was fun and frivolity, but they were living in the shadow of war. It was if they knew their time to be young and carefree was short, so they shouldn't waste it. World War II was raging when Wales was in high school. He not only knew what he would one day do but relished the prospect. He and his buddies, like all able-bodied high school boys in the early 1940s, felt a sense of duty. Wales felt it early.

The Japanese attacked Pearl Harbor on December 7, 1941. Wales was in ninth grade. The attack, which drew the U.S. into war, had a profound effect on him. He hungered to be of age to do what he could to get revenge on the Japanese.

"It was very personal to me. At the top of my priority list was to fight the Japanese and kill them," he said. "I wanted to seek my own individual revenge."

He would ride his bike without holding onto the handle bars, singing "Off we go, into the wild blue yonder..." Wales was, he said, fighting the war in his mind.

"The years of high school were really preparatory for me to go into the service," he said. "That's what I really wanted to do."

1943 AHS ROTC

Wales went to summer school over two summers in order to graduate early, finishing in December 1944. He and several others graduated five months ahead of their class. Wales gave the graduation speech at the small December commencement. He spoke of his and his friends' duty to defend this country and of what was ahead for them and America.

In Europe, the war was turning to the Allies' favor, and it seemed like only a few months before Germany would surrender. In the Pacific, however, years of bloody battles with the fanatical Japanese seemed likely.

Wales wanted to join the Navy. He figured it was the best and quickest way to fight the Japanese. Several of his friends joined him in that service branch.

Wales was leaving Amarillo behind. The world awaited. He was seventeen.

ADDITIONAL PHOTOS

Ninney, Mary Anne and me "27"

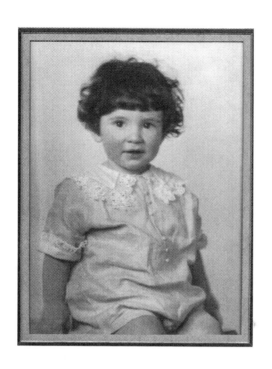

WM and Mary Ann Hall (Caldwell)

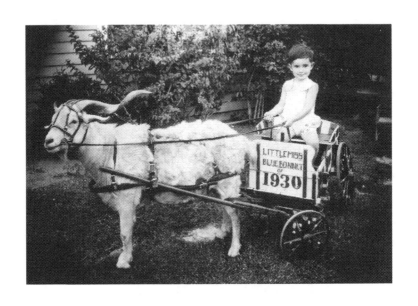

Pat Oles and WM

WM about 1934

1934 WM and Katy Madden

Pep with "Kanswer" "37"

1937 Wales Sr.

1943 Peewee Lanham and WM
Photo by B Hughes

Photo by B Hughes

The Gang on Bill Hughes' car
Photo by B Hughes

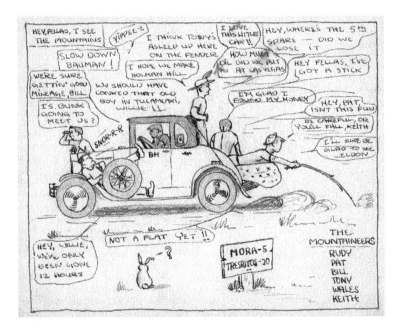

Illustration by Eldon Durrett, dec.

RESTLESS FOR WAR

When Wales enrolled at the University of Texas in January 1945, his head was barely into what was happening at the Forty Acres, and his heart surely wasn't in it. He and many other boys had graduated early from Amarillo High School the month before. Their intention had not been to go off to college but to fight for their country in World War II.

Wales was taking a freshman course load and, due to a lack of male students, was already pledging a fraternity, Phi Delta Theta. However, he was chafing at college life and longed to be somewhere on the high seas.

"I felt like my parents inadvertently were putting me in a position of dodging the service," he said. "I loved UT from the very beginning but felt like I shouldn't be there."

Wales composed a letter to send back home, telling his father that he was miserable. He wanted to join the Navy and fight, and if they didn't agree to let him drop out, he was going to leave anyway. They consented, feeling like they really didn't have a choice. Their son was serious.

Wales returned to Amarillo and quickly found out the fastest way into the Navy was induction in Dallas. So he, Eugene Lyons, and Mickey Graham hopped on a train heading to Dallas to take a physical and a simple battery of tests. They figured they would take the next train back to Amarillo and wait until they were called up.

After Wales and his buddies had finished all their preliminaries, enlistment officers came to the group and asked for volunteers to head to San Diego and Naval boot camp—right now. Wales raised his hand, as did Lyons and Graham. Just like that, they were heading west to California. Somewhere, perhaps El Paso, the train stopped long enough for Wales to phone home and break the news.

"I called my poor mother to tell her that her son was already in the Navy and headed for boot camp," Wales said. "She was devastated. I didn't realize how bad it would be for her, but it was a very thoughtless experience. She started sobbing.

"My dad got on the phone, and I don't think these were his exact words, but it was something to the effect of, 'You little son of a bitch, how are you going to get back to the house?' That was the beginning of my Navy career. If you can get more to the bottom than that, I've never heard of it."

Wales arrived in San Diego in February 1945, and many of his Amarillo friends were also there. Bill Hughes, the Hamilton twins, George Morris, as well as Lyons and Graham joined him. They were in different companies and rarely saw each other.

Wales flourished in basic training. For one thing, he was in excellent physical shape. Others would stumble and fall during drills, but Wales thought it was a lark.

One exercise required jumping off a fifty-foot tower into a pool, swimming under a moored rubber raft, then finishing the course. Lyons, in Wales' company, couldn't swim. They were lined up alphabetically with "L" next to "M." Wales had an idea.

"We called him 'Curly,' and I said, 'Curly, as we get on this platform, let me move in front of you, nobody will stop us, and let me jump in the water. I'll be down there when you come down, and I'll get you under and past that raft," Wales said. "It worked just perfectly. Curly still talks about that day and how he learned to swim."

When they would march, Wales was directly behind Lyons, as "Ma" follows "Ly." He was in the perfect position for some fun. Wales would intentionally kick the bottom of Lyons' foot on almost every right step, causing Lyons to occasionally lurch forward.

"The three-striper who was leading us would yell to Curly to cut out the horse play," Wales said. "Poor Curly. He wasn't doing anything."

Wales loved everything about the ninety-day boot camp: the camaraderie, the challenges, the adventure. He was ready for more.

After boot camp, he took a leave to go back to Amarillo for friend Tony Martin's wedding. Wales was standing with the bride and groom not long after they had been pronounced man and wife, and in the rice-throwing celebration, some rice stuck in his ear. "It hurt like hell," he said.

Wales boarded a train to return to California, but he got off in Clovis at 1:00 a.m. for a Navy quartermaster to get the rice out of his ear. After the pesky grain of rice was removed, Wales spent the night on a bench at the train station. He left the next morning on another train bound for San Francisco. When he arrived, his assigned ship had already left.

"But the [alternate] ship I was assigned to was even better because it was faster," he said. "I wanted the smallest, fastest ship to get into the war, and this was it. It really fit my needs very well."

USS Lipan cir. late 1940's

The ship was the U.S.S. ATF-85 *Lipan*, a seagoing tugboat. An armed 205-foot ship, its purpose was to remove damaged boats and rafts from the beach and pull them back into the water. As a quartermaster, Wales was responsible for watch-to-watch navigation and for maintaining and preparing charts.

"I knew I could get on one of those rafts to help pull a boat off the beach in Japan," he said. "While doing that, abandon that boat and grab a Japanese rifle and go in and fight. That was my total plan how I was going to get on shore."

Going AWOL to get into battle?

"Yeah, sure," Wales said.

It was on the *Lipan* that Wales was again color blind when he offered to bunk with the black crew members of the kitchen detail. Wales went on board the ship in San Francisco at midnight. The boatswain's mate directed him where to go. He dropped into the crew quarters.

The bunks were four high with sixty sleeping in crew quarters. In the corner were four black sailors, but the bunks were not full. Madden asked if he could sleep where the blacks were.

"He [the boatswain's mate] said, 'What are you, a n—lover?' I said I just wanted to know if I could sleep over there. He said, 'Hell, I guess you can.' I went to bed in uniform. The next morning the word was out what they had on board. You can imagine people were not too cordial to me. Again, I was pretty physical, and there weren't too many people I was afraid of changing their minds if I had to. That went on for maybe a week. I never felt like it was anything to be ashamed of, being a friend of a black."

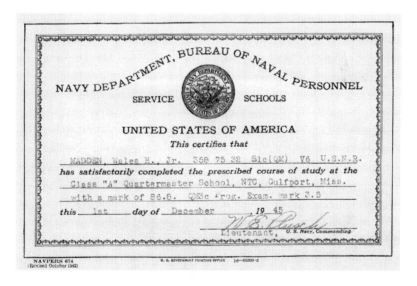

Quartermaster's Certificate

There was something to be ashamed of, or at least embarrassed about, because of one incident when Wales was quartermaster on deck. He was on his first midwatch, from midnight to 4:00 a.m., when he saw the distant flashing of dot, dash, dot, dash, dot, dash, dash. That meant another ship wanted a return signal and then to relay a message.

Wales flashed back his light. The distant light kept flashing. A thirty-six-inch arc light needed to be turned on, but the engineering officer would have to be awakened to turn on power for the arc light.

"Oooh, I didn't even know if you had to take off your hat when you go into the officers' quarters," he said.

Wales went down the ladder, knocked on the engineering officer's bedroom door, and told him the power needed to be turned on for the arc light because a ship needed the *Lipan* to relay a message. The grumbling officer stumbled up to the very top of the ship. The arc light went on, and Wales flashed back to the distant light.

"Where are you sending to, sailor?" the officer asked.

"Sir, over there," Wales replied.

"You stupid son of a bitch. That's the Oakland Air Base beacon light!"

USS Lipan arc light and crow's nest-center right

The *Lipan* soon set sail for Pearl Harbor, which was to be its base of operations. It was an interesting arrival, to say the least. Wales was a green sailor, and it was his first major mooring. Ships were moored ahead of the *Lipan* at Pearl. Each ship had a mooring line from the stern to keep them against the dock. The *Lipan* was coming in pretty fast. Wales was at the helm.

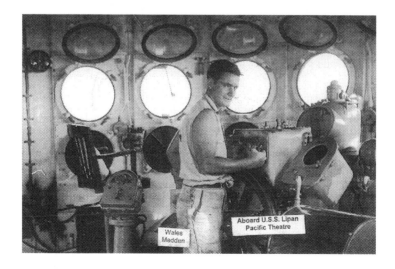

At the helm

"I said, 'Sir, we're approaching at a rapid speed. Sir, we're approaching at a rapid speed-CAPTAIN!'" Wales said. "He [the captain] was sitting in his chair. Then he said, 'Reverse! All power, reverse!' The engines switched and starting slowing down, but it was too late. The ship we hit had a rubber rear bumper. People were sitting on the fan tail, and some got knocked over, fell down. That was a flaw in his intelligence."

The captain asked Wales not to mention the incident in his report. There was the quartermaster's log and the officer-of-the-deck's log. The two logs didn't agree.

"I told him once that I was going to law school," Wales said, "and he told me I wasn't smart enough to go to law school. He was probably right."

Lifelong high school chum, Bill Hughes, was also in the Navy at Pearl, but he spent much of his time as a lifeguard. Wales and Hughes would spend their weekend liberty together in Honolulu.

Wales had hungered to join the Navy and was eager for battle in the late summer of 1945, even though he was not quite eighteen years old. With the U.S. closing in on Japan, a bloody invasion loomed. The *Lipan* went out daily from Pearl to practice maneuvers for the likely invasion. Most knew it was a matter of time.

Even in his patriotism Wales felt a sense of vulnerability and mortality, an understanding that there was something bigger and grander than himself and this life. He felt a calling to God during that time. Most men felt a sense of a higher calling, of something spiritual, during times of crisis. There's a saying that there are no atheists in foxholes, but that trivializes the transformation Wales experienced on a day in August 1945.

During quartermaster school and at Pearl, when the situation permitted, Wales would attend both a Protestant service and a Catholic service, back to back, hoping to understand their different approaches to Christ. While at Pearl, Wales didn't have every Sunday off. When he was on ship, instead of going to church, he would go up to the top bridge, where the search light was, and say a prayer.

"The first time, I felt cold chills go down my back," he said. "I thought, 'Gee whiz, here we are about to do all this fighting, and I don't know where I'm going to end up.' I can remember getting on my knees. I don't remember what I prayed, but it was something like, 'Oh, Lord, give me a hand here. This may be it.' I felt a peace that I still feel. I felt very clearly Christ's presence. That was when I felt my conversion to Christianity."

The atomic bombs dropped on Hiroshima and Nagasaki in August 1945 forced Japan to surrender days later. That ended the war and precluded the invasion of Japan. War planners said an invasion would have cost millions of lives on both sides. Although it meant that Wales and the rest of the armed forces would be spared the invasion, Wales felt a little let down. He had yearned for personal revenge against the Japanese since the Pearl Harbor attack in 1941 when he was fourteen years old.

"I don't remember anyone who was as enthusiastic as I was about invading Japan," he said. "I wanted to do whatever I could do to get into the fight. I really felt let down. Here I was focusing on getting into the fight literally and not able to do that now. Things went along so fast. My thinking, though, was probably immature."

Looking back seventy years, Wales doesn't have the same driven patriotism he once had. He doubts he would jump on the back of a tugboat, willing to risk his life for the situation the United States is in today.

The Navy discharged nearly all sailors as quickly as possible. Wales estimated it was about a month before he was discharged. Most of the Amarillo sailors returned shortly, arriving by train at the Santa Fe station where they were greeted by a huge crowd with Wales' friend Boone Pickens among the crowd.

Home from the War
Photo by Bill Hughes

Now Wales could take a deep breath, see his parents again, feel at home, but not for too long. The University of Texas lay ahead. This time Wales' heart *was* in it.

1945 "Two Navy vets headed to UT" Pat Oles and WM

About 1945-Bill Hughes, WM and Rudy Bauman

RETURN TO THE FORTY ACRES

The country was in a post-war boom in early 1946. Men were returning home, reuniting with families and girlfriends, searching for jobs, restarting their lives. For many, like Wales Madden, that meant returning to college.

Austin, Texas, was teeming with students that year. It was nothing like it had been when Wales first attended UT. Now it was exploding with students, many coming back from World War II, anxious to put a war behind them and an education ahead of them.

Finding a place to stay in Austin was not easy. Enrollment was almost doubling. Infrastructure was stretched to the limits. Lodging was hit-or-miss, mostly miss. Wales, however, had a bit of an "in." His father was on the board of directors of an Amarillo bank and knew some Austin bankers. One of the bankers and his wife were living with her mother. She was a widow who had an extra bedroom and bath.

So, Wales had a bed, but he also had a roommate, John Douglas Pittman from Hereford. Pittman's father and Wales, Sr., were good friends. Their sons didn't know each other, but their fathers arranged the accommodations. Pittman was six-foot-two. One bed. This may not work.

"We slept in a bed-no, we occupied a bed-for one night, and John Douglas was a great guy. I said, 'Get out a quarter. We're going to match, and the loser is out on the street,'" said Wales, who won the coin toss. "Pat Oles, who was smaller, showed up that very day. We stayed together for six months and shared a double bed, with no air conditioning."

In Wales' brief stay at UT before enlisting in the Navy, he had become a member of Phi Delta Theta fraternity. Upon his return, he helped many of his old Amarillo buddies to join the Phi Delts. Among them were Rudy and Bobby Bauman, Keith James, Pat Babb, Jack Shelton, and Pat Oles.

Wales entered Texas intending to study law. It was an easy decision, one influenced by the work of his attorney grandfather and father.

"I always wanted to," he said. "It was a family tradition to me. I thought it would be fun. To be a lawyer seemed right down my alley. There was an aura about it that appealed to me. In life, good lawyers are dadgum important, and I wanted to be one. Law has always been fascinating to me."

Wales' grades may not have been a four point, but they were good enough. He was a member of the honorary arts and sciences fraternity, freshman honor society Phi Eta Sigma, and government honor society, but he missed Phi Beta Kappa because of a "C" in Spanish. He enjoyed government, history, and English, especially English literature. At some point, he changed his major from business to government.

"I couldn't understand accounting at all. In fact, I dropped out of accounting after three weeks, and I couldn't understand Spanish," Wales said. "This wonderful Spanish lady teacher said, 'Mr. Madden, I want to see you after class.' She told me, 'You still have a "C" in Spanish. Why don't you drop the course before you take another test?' I said 'Yes, ma'am! Adios, amigos.'"

The classroom was just a portion of the Longhorn experience. Wales was active socially, in service organizations, and in student government. Grass didn't grow under his feet. There were never quite enough hours in the day.

Wales was Abbot (president) of the Friar Society, one of the highest student honor societies on campus. He was also president of the Interfraternity Council and Foreman of the Cowboys, a service organization and longtime fixture at Texas.

"I think I got elected because I was straw boss-I kept good notes at meetings," he said. "My notes were so funny and corny that everyone thought they'd like to hear them. I kind of have a sense of humor that gets away from you if you're not careful."

1947 Texas Cowboys

It was in the Cowboys that Wales became friends with Tom Landry. Wales also became friends with fellow students Barefoot Sanders and Frank Erwin, men who would later be known across the state, but no other name would ring with the public like Landry's, as he was destined to become the legendary coach of the Dallas Cowboys. During the war, Landry was a B-17 bomber co-pilot in Europe. Now he was defensive back and fullback for the Longhorns and likely was held in a little higher regard by his student peers than Wales was. Both Landry and Wales pledged the Cowboys, but they each received a little bit different treatment.

"He was a superman, just a superman, and we were in the same pledge class," Wales said of Landry. "We were alphabetically arranged out in the country, and they were feeding us. I didn't drink any alcoholic beverages at all, but they started feeding us. Garlic, tobacco, beer, all this stuff. The new pledges would stand there, and the old members would come by and stuff your mouth. They'd come to Landry and say, 'Hey, Tom, great game, great game. You were really something. Oh, Tom, you don't need to eat this. Here, Madden, take his.' They would double my order. He never forgot that and I didn't either, but he was just a wonderful man."

Barefoot Sanders, Frank Erwin, and noted political liberal Ronnie Dugger were among Wales' fraternity brothers.

Sanders would become a district judge and counsel to President Lyndon Johnson, as well as a state representative and Democratic candidate for the U.S. Senate in 1972. While a university student, Sanders was president of the UT student body, and Wales helped him get there, almost to his detriment. Wales was campaigning for his friend when disaster nearly struck.

"I almost got arrested at midnight one night outside the Co-op on Guadalupe, painting bare feet on the sidewalk during his campaign," Wales said. "I saw a squad car coming down from where the police station was, from the south. I didn't want to hang around with a bucket of paint."

Bruce Meador, the other culprit with Wales, was too big, too heavy, and too slow. The cops got him.

"They weren't about to catch me. I ran north and turned at the Co-op and ran into an alley," Wales said. "In the meantime, my good buddy had been put in jail. I had to get someone from the fraternity to go with me, and you can imagine how easy that was. 'Here it's midnight and you want me to go down there to the jail with you to get him out?'"

Frank Erwin helped Wales to be elected as Interfraternity Council president. They were friends as students, but Wales did not agree with some of his tough stances when he cast an immense shadow over the campus as a member of the board of regents from 1963 to 1975, serving as chairman from 1966 to 1971. Erwin, whose name has been on the Events Center in Austin since 1977, often ran things with an iron fist.

"Erwin and I were really good friends, but philosophically, I did not agree with him on most politics," he said. "Whatever liberal was, he was, yet we were good friends. Frank got mad at a dean in the college of liberal arts and wanted him fired. I was involved because I was on this committee under which this dean served.

"I told Erwin I would fight him until hell froze over before I would support him in firing this teacher. We preserved this teacher, but not very long afterwards, he quit and went to Harvard. In spite of this and some other things, I never challenged that Frank wanted what was best for the university."

Ronnie Dugger was the editor of the *Daily Texan* in 1950-51. He went on to become the founding editor of the *Texas Observer*, an influential liberal publication. Called the "godfather of progressive journalism in Texas" by the *Austin American-Statesman*, Dugger is likely the most influential liberal journalist in the state's history.

"He and I were just buddies," said Wales of Dugger, who was in the same class of the Friars as Wales. "He and I did not lie to each other. We disagreed on a lot of things, but I never downgraded or degraded his beliefs, and he didn't mine. He was a bright, bright guy who really cared for his causes, even though I thought a lot of them were squirrelly."

However, the person Wales met who clearly stood above all others, who stole his heart and changed his life, was a pretty co-ed from Midland whom he initially tried to tell to quiet down in the library. Her name was Abbie Cowden. It may not have been love at first sight, but it was certainly no later than the second sight. Although they would marry in 1952, the relationship did not get off to a real smooth beginning, with Wales dodging an unfortunate, though accidental, incident at one point.

Wales was in his third year at Texas when he and Pat Oles went to the library to study. Abbie and a sorority sister in Kappa Kappa Gamma, were also there, opposite Wales and Pat. The girls were giggling and making a small ruckus.

"What can we do?" Wales said.

"Tell them to shut up!" Oles said.

So, Wales poked his head around a small partition and asked them to keep it down, that he and Pat were serious students and their noise was bothersome.

"I turned around to Pat and said, 'Gosh, she's cute,' and that's where it started," he said.

Wales was slightly acquainted with a friend of Abbie's. So, it was relayed to Abbie who Wales was, that he was a Phi Delt and a self-described "smart ass." He let it be known he'd like a date with Abbie, and a date was arranged.

To take Abbie out, Wales used the car that was shared among five guys. Being a teetotaler, Wales' idea of a generous date was an ice cream sundae. They went to Weary Willie's Ice Cream Parlor on Congress Avenue.

"Bless her heart. We got our ice cream and came back to the car," Wales said. "She got a cone and I got one in a cup. When I started off, she dropped her cone on this plaid seat. She's such a sensitive, caring person, and there she is dropping her ice cream cone on my seat. We had to get some napkins. I drove her back to the Kappa house. The future was not too predictable at that point, but I just knew somehow she was going to be the girl. I really did."

Wales and Abbie became steady boyfriend and girlfriend, sharing together what little free time they each had. Wales even went to Midland to visit her parents. Then, along came "THE PICTURE."

BARTON'S 1950 attractions are sunbathing — and UT beauties like Ysleta Leissner, Wales Madden is the boy.

1950 Miss Texas and WM
Source: The Daily Texan

While dating and beginning to grow serious with Abbie, Wales met Miss Texas, Ysleta Leisner, in an innocent way. The two were among a group at Barton Springs. A photographer asked them to lie on their stomachs for a photo. Wales remembers a silly grin. That was harmless enough—until it wasn't.

The photo appeared in the *Daily Texan*. Wales and Abbie had not seen each other for several days when Wales went to the Kappa house to take her to Sunday breakfast. The girls in the lobby were noticeably cool to Wales. Then the situation grew worse.

"On the front page of the *Daily Texan* was that picture, and it said, 'Miss Texas and boyfriend.' I didn't even have a name," Wales said. "That didn't go over real well, but the picture made it all the way to Midland where Abbie lived. Her folks saw it, and that necessitated a drive to Midland to talk with her folks.

"I told them, 'I'm sorry about this, but I'm in love with your daughter, and I'm very serious about it.'"

Abbie had an aunt who liked Wales. She helped convince Wales' future in-laws that he was an honorable man who had been the victim of being in the wrong place at the wrong time, circumstances compounded by a misleading photo caption.

"I will say Miss Texas was a dadgummed fine gal, and I saw her at the fiftieth reunion just several years ago. She had a paralysis," Wales said.

Miss Texas didn't sway Wales a bit in the romance department, even though he had to do some quick maneuvering and apologizing. There was only one Abbie Cowden.

Wales liked Abbie's total honesty, her soft side of caring about people and animals. She didn't drink or smoke. Former valedictorian of her Midland High School class, she was bright. She would become a renowned artist. Abbie's personality was open and friendly.

"I never met anyone like her," Wales said.

Wales had Abbie at his side when he ran for student body president. He had been asked to run, and he felt it was an opportunity he could not let pass by. Wales had worked on the campaign of fraternity brother Barefoot Sanders two years previously. Lloyd Hand was president following Sanders.

Madden for President campaign car

The campaign was wide open in 1951. Abbie and Wales were becoming serious, and she was concerned that she would not be seeing him as much.

"She said, 'Does that mean we won't have any time together?'" Wales said. "And I said, 'No, no, no, but it does mean I'm going to have to go make speeches to all the sorority houses.'"

Two years earlier bare feet had been painted for Sanders; this time figures of whales were being painted for Wales. They went on sidewalks, around the Co-Op, places that were frowned upon.

Wales' platform called for paving Nineteenth Street, which is now Martin Luther King Boulevard. He also emphasized student involvement and participation in activities to make for a better university.

"Pretty heady stuff," he said.

During the session of the state Legislature, Wales led a movement to defend and protect the Permanent University Fund. The PUF was a sovereign wealth fund created by the state as an endowment strictly for the University of Texas and Texas A&M. Wales had a secretary, paid for by the Student Association, write letters to groups around the state to support the PUF.

"Landslide Wales" won by fewer than 1,000 votes, one of the few fraternity members to be elected to be the head of student government at the beginning of the second half of the twentieth century.

Although Wales' time as president was briefer than he expected it to be, he left his mark by appointing blacks to campus leadership roles. He remembered the way the Madden's maid, Beulah Wells, was treated in Amarillo during the 1930s, and the segregation of black sailors on his tugboat in the 1940s. It just wasn't right or fair. Wales made the first appointment of a black student to a student body committee about the same time the UT Law School admitted its first black student. Of course, that doesn't even register sixty-five years later, but it was significant in 1951.

"I talked to several girls on the committee to see if they had any problem with a black student working with them," he said. "I didn't care about the boys, but I felt like girls came from different cultures. I found out that no one had a problem at all. Not a big deal—but a big deal."

In those days, if accepted, students could enroll in UT's Law School before they completed a bachelor's degree. Wales was in law school by his third year at UT, coinciding with the enrollment of Heman Sweatt as the first black law student after he had won a lawsuit, *Sweatt v. Painter*, against the university.

One morning, as Wales was about to enter the law school building, he saw the charred embers of what had been a burning cross. He could smell the ashes. It bothered him. He went inside to get a metal waste basket to clean up the remains.

"All of a sudden, I realized there were four, five, six to eight people out there helping me," he said. "We scooped up those ashes and were ashamed of it. It was like, 'Come on, what kind of coward would do this?'"

Wales had to relinquish his student body presidency before his term expired because he flunked a federal taxation class in law school. That proved to be a bit humbling.

"I had to give it up," he said. "That was pretty embarrassing because the independents could say these 'frat rats' aren't worthy to be serving in this job. Wilson Foreman (vice-president) took over and did a great job."

Wales had about ninety hours of college classes when he entered law school. The first year went toward earning his B.A. degree in government. Law school was an up-and-down challenge, its rigors and demands shaping Wales into an attorney. Professors like Gray Thoron, Charlie Meyers, Kenneth Woodward, and Joe Sneed challenged him, and the very approachable, very bright, very dignified Dean Page Keeton made an impression.

When Wales was running for student body president, some jokester painted a rather large sign of a character that resembled Professor Thoron. It said, "Me and my hoss, Tex, is fur Wales Madden." When Wales found out, he went into damage control mode. He sailed into the dignified Thoron's class, intent on setting the record straight, but it was Thoron who spoke first.

"He said, 'Mr. Madden, tell me about 'my hoss, Tex,'" Wales said. "He kept me on my feet for an hour about cases I hadn't even read. We were close, close friends. I think I was pretty much a smart ass, and he knew it."

Law school became much more difficult when Wales, Sr., fell ill in Amarillo. As one of Amarillo's top attorneys, the elder Madden cast a long shadow in the city. He and his father, S.H. Madden, were influential in Wales, Jr.'s, choosing law as a career.

Wales spent time in Amarillo with his father in St. Anthony's Hospital and was there when he died, leaving a hole in Wales' life. Both men would have enjoyed practicing law together, at the same time and in the same city.

"It was an emotional time," Wales said. "My mother was not a strong person. Of course, I loved my father. His impact on me was integrity and determination. He was smarter than I was, but not in dealing with people. I was more of a people person."

Eventually, Wales worked his way through just about every obstacle at the University of Texas, through undergraduate and law school, through the social and service aspects. All that remained was to study for the bar exam-or so he thought.

He was finishing up his final semester of law school, but that seemed like merely a formality. Most of Wales' time and energy were focused on the bar exam. Yes, there was a tough visiting law professor from the East teaching a Creditors' Rights course, and, yes, he didn't really like Wales, but so be it.

"I hardly knew what a creditors' right was," Wales said, "because I was studying so much for the bar exam."

At the end of the semester, Wales and a fraternity brother took a brief break. They drove to Amarillo, and, from there, headed to Gunnison, Colorado, to do a little fly-fishing. They hadn't even put their lines in the river when Wales received a call from his roommate back in Austin. He had flunked Creditors' Rights, and the law professor had gone back East. If Wales didn't graduate law school, there would be no bar exam and no law career, at least for the time being.

"I immediately did all I could to get back to Austin," he said. "Train, bus, car. I went non-stop. I needed three hours to graduate, and I had to find a course I could take right away. I tell you, that humanized me a great deal."

He enrolled in a course, earned the needed passing grade, then focused on the bar exam.

Life as a student at the University of Texas was coming to an end, yet it was to be the springboard for so much of his life. A new wife, a family, and a promising career in his hometown lay ahead.

Additional Photos

Alma Faye Cowden baby photo

"Prissy" Alma Faye

1949 150 lb wrestling champs, WM left.

1950 Phi Delta Theta formal

NEW FAMILY, NEW CAREER

Wales had the end of law school in his sights in 1951 and 1952, but he had something else in his sights as well-the hand of Abbie Cowden. Not long after his telling her to keep the noise down in the University of Texas library and her dropping her ice cream on his car seat on their first date, Wales knew she would one day be his wife. It was just a question of when.

Wales was never one to do anything in a conventional way, including proposing marriage. He bought an engagement ring and hatched a plan.

Wales, Sr., had already been slowed by his first stroke when Abbie came to Amarillo for a visit in the Madden home on Ong Street. Wales, Jr., and Abbie were alone there when Wales implemented his plan.

"I had the ring in my pocket, and we were sitting by the fire," he said. "It was in my handkerchief. She knew I was in love with her, and vice versa. As I got up, I put my hand in my pocket and pulled out my handkerchief, and I let the ring fall on the carpet.

"She didn't know that was coming. She said, 'Ohhhhhh.' Had I been her, I would have kicked me right in the teeth, but she didn't do that. I was still kind of a smart aleck."

She said yes, of course. Abbie probably would have been surprised if her boyfriend had not tried something a bit different. They set a wedding date after law school graduation, but there was a bit of drama when a visiting law professor flunked Wales in that pesky Creditors' Rights class that last semester. However, after a scramble to find another class to take-and pass-he was soon out of law school, headed for the bar exam and a wedding.

Wales and Abbie were married in November 1952 at the First Baptist Church in her hometown of Midland. It was a social event in the oil town. The honeymoon, though, not so much.

WM, Katy and Wales Sr.

Katy Madden, Abbie, Clyde
and Jessie Cowden

They went to Acapulco. They *drove* to Acapulco in Abbie's Cadillac. Wales soon learned it was not quite as easy as jumping into the car with his old fraternity brothers for a cross-country trek.

"At every hotel, you could see people lining up to unpack the car. She had enough bags for people to hand them off to each other. I didn't have enough money to tip them all," Wales said. "Finally, I said, 'Honey, just leave the bags in the car. You don't have to take everything out. Just leave them in car.' We had no room in the backseat." Wales remembers he needed "barely a bag" for what he had brought.

Driving may not have been the best idea, but it was the only means of travel they could afford since they were honeymooning on a limited budget. When they arrived at each succeeding hotel, they were so tired they just went to sleep.

Eventually, the two returned to Amarillo, Wales' hometown, where he began work as an attorney with the Shamrock Oil and Gas Corporation.

He had several job offers elsewhere, including one from a friend of his father's with an oil company in Fort Worth. Wales had always wanted to practice law with his father, but Wales, Sr., had died during his son's last year of law school. Still, he felt drawn to return to his hometown, this time with a new wife.

1953 newly weds

"I like Amarillo-I still do," he said. "Gosh, being born, going to school, going to the Navy from here. Nothing dramatic or romantic. This was my home. Being on all these boards across the state was wonderful, but this is my home."

Shamrock president and chairman Harold Dunn, a staunch Texas Aggie, had spread the word that he'd like to hire the newly minted graduate of UT Law School. Wales quickly accepted and was assigned to work under the stately Ray Johnson. Johnson, Wales said, was "a lovable man and a good lawyer." Johnson's assistant was Ed Selecman.

"Ed told me the job would be waiting for me if I didn't flunk anymore," said Wales, referring to his ill-fated Creditors' Rights class at Texas.

Wales joined another attorney, J. Avery Rush, who was his immediate superior. They shared an office at Eighth Avenue and Tyler Street, and on more than one occasion, they shared the men's room. For whatever reason, these two happened to use the facilities at the same time nearly every day. The men's room had two toilets and two urinals.

"People would notice we'd go in the restroom at the same time, and I can just imagine what people were saying behind our backs," Wales said, "but Avery said, 'What do you think we can do?'

"I had an idea. We'd memorize all the state capitals. Then while we're sitting there, we can quiz each other. He'd say, 'Oklahoma,' and I'd say, 'Oklahoma City,' and so on. Finally, there were pretty bad stories coming out from people who just went in there to take care of their business. Here they were, two guys on the toilets quizzing each other about the state capitals. I thought it was great fun."

Wales' earliest duties at Shamrock included obtaining oil and gas leases as well as practicing law. He made a number of trips to Kansas to check the records in an area. Wales didn't evaluate geology, only ownership. Based on his recommendations, Shamrock often sent Wales out to buy the leases. Shamrock put together leases in southwestern Kansas that turned into a huge gas field.

"I especially enjoyed working with the people at Shamrock. They were bright, fun. That was a young company with some legendary accomplishments."

As Wales was starting a new career, there was also a new family but not without initial heartache. A young daughter died the day after birth because of a blood disorder, RH negative factor. Friends remember her as "a pretty little girl with black hair."

"We were very discouraged because our doctor told us we would not be able to have a child who would live," Wales said.

Unless a pregnancy would endanger Abbie, they were determined to try for a family, but it was a nervous time. In 1955, Abbie became pregnant a second time, and she and Wales made several trips to Boston to see a specialist.

Fortunately, this child was born healthy. Wales Madden III was born on August 5, 1955. A sister, Straughn, known to all as "Tawney," was born on January 25, 1958.

Wales, Jr.'s, father had been focused on building a career during the Depression, and there was some distance between him and his son. Wales, Sr., didn't have much time to be with his son, although they did make trips to Almont, Colorado, where he taught Wales, Jr., to fish for trout. Wales, Jr.'s, young son was the namesake of his grandfather and father, and the two of them were close from the beginning.

While a student at the University of Texas, Wales began attending the University Presbyterian Church which was near the Phi Delta Theta house. He was baptized in that church. Abbie was raised in the Baptist church. After they married and moved to Amarillo, Wales and Abbie joined First Presbyterian Church where Wales was soon elected an elder. According to him, he was elected because of his "innate nosiness." Being in his late twenties, Wales is believed to be the youngest elder ever elected in that church.

During the late 1950s and early 1960s, other young married couples from the church often gathered in the Madden home for a time of Bible study and fellowship. Wales and Abbie's children were raised in the church, and they knew where they would be on Sunday mornings, unless they were sick or out of town.

Wales and Abbie shared the adventures of the outdoors and a love of fishing with their children. The family took frequent trips to the Colorado mountains, to California, and elsewhere.

"I can remember when he [Wales III] was five or six years old, and we'd go to Colorado. We'd stop by the peak outside Capulin, New Mexico, and every time we'd go by that peak, I'd tell him that's one of the world's largest extinct volcanoes," Wales said.

"He would make me take him up that dadgum road again. Then we'd get out and look down, and if you've been there, it's all overgrown. He'd sneak up on the edge up of it, and I'd yell, 'I think it's erupting! I think it's erupting!' And we'd go, 'Ahhhhhh!' It's a wonder he's normal."

"I'm not normal," Wales III said. "It's no wonder I'm not normal."

For Wales III, it was the trips when he was young that were memorable, for one reason or another. One of the earliest was a trip to Midland, his mother's hometown. On this occasion they flew, which turned out to be an unfortunate choice because of his airsickness.

"I was small enough to be carried off the plane because I was big-time sick," Wales III said. "I warned Dad that I was going to throw up. He said, 'No, you're not; no, you're not.' So we're walking off the plane, and I managed to unleash it all over the back of his shirt."

There were fishing trips and learning how to ski when Wales III was just three years old. He remembers using the rope tow at Santa Fe. There were hunting trips with Boone Pickens, and trips to Texas football games.

"We didn't fly much. It was all marathon road trips," Wales III said. "You couldn't drink much water. We weren't stopping."

Going to California was an annual summer trip. The Maddens would visit Wales, Jr.'s, aunt in San Diego, and they would stay at the Hotel del Coronado. Those vacations often included a trip north to Los Angeles and Disneyland.

1960 Knott's Berry Farm

*1962 Disneyland; Tamneys,
Babbs & Maddens*

On any trip Wales, Jr., had a three-warning limit. If someone was warned three times in one day, there would be no swimming in the hotel pool that night-and they *always* had to stop at a place with a pool. The family traveled in a station wagon, with the luggage in the back, the middle seat folded down, and a large pad on the floorboard. Often, vacations included Wales III's and Tawney's friends who now have families of their own.

When Wales III was about ten and Tawney seven, they broke a record for miles logged on a trip. From Amarillo, they flew along the west coast of South America:

1965 Machu Picchu,

Ecuador; Lima, Peru; Santiago, Chile; the Panama Canal. They saw guinea pigs being grilled in Ecuador, which made an impression on the young boy and girl. Wales III got sick while in Argentina.

"I was careful not to carry him on my shoulder again," quipped Wales, Jr.

More often than not when Wales, Jr., went to Austin, whether for business or for Texas sporting events, his family went with him.

Wales III said, "We'd go to parties, and there would be people like John Connally, Lloyd Bentsen, LBJ. John Connally was one of the most amazing people I've ever met. He was a 'crowd-parter.' His physical presence was so different.

"When you grow up knowing people like that and seeing your dad with them, it is pretty impressive as a kid. I hated going to the adult cocktail parties and pre-game events at UT as a kid, but looking back, it was an opportunity for Tawney and me to get to know those that very few people ever get the chance to meet. LBJ had the biggest ears I've ever seen. They were huge."

Tawney acquired her nickname from her brother, who was older by two and a half years, because he could not pronounce his little sister's name. She was named after an uncle of Abbie's. Tawney thought Straughn must have been a favorite uncle, but her mother never really knew him. She just liked the name. For Wales III "Straughn" was a mouthful. His pronunciation produced a slurred version, more like "Tawney," and it stuck. Perhaps Tawney also could have been called "Me Too," since she insisted on tagging along to every event.

"My poor brother," Tawney said. "They'd go hunting, and I probably threw a fit until I got to go, too. I'd go dove and quail hunting, and Daddy taught me to do that. My dad gave me a love for nature and the outdoors and always to be aware of where you are. It helps in seeing animals and birds and learning what kind of tracks we were seeing."

Wales, Jr., taught Tawney some Biblical lessons that weren't necessarily directly from the Bible—like not to assume, whether about people or situations, and to make sure to gather all the facts. That's in Proverbs 13. The other was no matter the job-even if it was scooping poop or pulling weeds-to do it with everything you had. That's from Colossians 3.

"But I was definitely, and still am, 'Daddy's Girl,'" Tawney said. "He loves me unconditionally and supports everything I do. When I was young, that made my trust in God so easily transferred, having had a dad who loved me like that. I understood God's love so much better than a lot of people because of my dad."

For Tawney a favorite story about her dad happened in about the second grade when she was in Bluebirds, an organization similar to the Girl Scouts. It was the 1960s, and Wales, Jr., traveled frequently then. He was on business in Germany when the Bluebirds were to have an end-of-the-year banquet.

"I was so sad he wasn't going to be there. I'd be one of the few who didn't have their dads there," she said, "and I went to the banquet thinking I was going to be Bluebird of the Year."

Two things surprised her. A mild surprise was that she wasn't Bluebird of the Year, but the bigger surprise was that her dad made it to the banquet. He flew to Amarillo, went to the banquet, and then flew back to Germany. You think that didn't make an impression on a young daughter?

As they are for Wales III, the summer trips are seared in Tawney's memory. This was decades before video games, iPods, and other electronic devices to entertain kids. What they had for entertainment was their dad who spun tall tales for hours about white stallions, bald eagles, and anything else he could conjure up.

"We'd stop at historical markers, and he was such a history buff that he'd know the history of that area," she said. "But not all the traveling was fun, at least not for my mom. She would always complain because it seemed like we stayed in the cheapest motels possible, and that was not my mother. I remember she'd get in there and start washing out the bathtub."

The family made frequent trips to Austin for fundraising events or meetings and especially to watch the Longhorns play. The trip down was often a briefing on that year's top football players.

"You had to know players' numbers. Number 16 was James Street. He'd quiz us, and you better know all the stats," she said.

It was understood, or at least inferred, by both Wales III and Tawney that a college education would be achieved at a certain university in Austin. If not, then good luck finding someone to pay for it.

"I was a senior at Tascosa," Tawney said, "and I had a lot of friends who were going to Oklahoma. I asked my dad if I could just go look at the campus with them. He said, 'Fine, you can go look, but if you go there, your scholarship is revoked.' I didn't even go look."

Wales, Jr., was sorta, kinda serious about that point but usually not about many others with his children. Yes, there were the stories and the lessons and the expectations, but his sense of humor was-and is-a constant.

"He can find humor in everything," Tawney said. "Growing up, I thought the point of telling a story was to get someone to believe something that wasn't true. He was constantly pulling tricks on people. But my perception was he never took humor too far. Usually the prank was on him."

ORANGE REMAINED IN HIS BLOOD

If anyone thought Wales Madden would put the University of Texas aside once he graduated from law school and began working in his hometown of Amarillo, well, they didn't know him too well. Forget Texas, the university where he met his wife, nurtured lifelong friendships, was educated in law, and grew into a man? Not likely. If anything, his love for and involvement with UT grew as he got older.

It was just a few years after graduation, 1957 to be exact, when Wales became a member of the UT Committee of 75. The committee was formed as the university was approaching its centennial celebration in 1975.

"That was really a promotion of UT," Wales said. "The leadership did not feel proper recognition had been given to UT for years, that we were a better school than given credit for. The focus was more on the academic side. I think they turned to me because of my experience. The people who were on that committee were really the wheelers and dealers of the university."

One year later, Wales was elected to the board of regents of Amarillo College. He had had an appreciation for the importance of education for a long time, and he knew the role that AC played in the city.

"I was so delighted by that," he said. "I thought it was vital for the city of Amarillo to have a school that people could enter easily to start off their career. The future of our country depends on the quality and availability of higher education. That's the way societies and civilizations grow. I preach that every time I have a chance."

It was not a long tenure on the AC board-two years to be exact. In 1959, he received a call from Texas Governor Price Daniel's office with an offer that he would never have considered refusing. He was asked to become a regent of the University of Texas.

A group within the UT Ex-Students Association believed that since graduating from law school, Wales had been overlooked and some of his ideas ignored. In the opinion of many, few people were more active or more qualified to serve on UT's highest ranking board than Wales. Without Wales' knowing it, they lobbied Governor Daniel on behalf of their influential friend, who was only thirty-one at the time.

"I finally knew about it when an assistant in Governor Daniel's office called me and said, 'Congratulations!'" Wales said. "I didn't even know for what. I knew that was a tremendous honor and one many people would grin at because I was so young, but those who knew me in school knew I worked damn hard at it."

The phone call actually came when Wales was in court in Dumas, and Abbie was there with him. The first regents' meeting was the next day in Austin. They quickly returned to Amarillo, gathered a change of clothes, and headed south. They arrived in Austin early that morning and checked into a hotel. Wales showered and shaved for the 9:00 a.m. meeting.

"I was a little intimidated," he said. "They were introducing me, and I was shaking hands with all of them. I was obviously very pleased and proud to be with them. They were all very polite, but it was kind of like, 'What in the hell are *you* doing here?'"

Wales was well-prepared for his first meeting. He later thought some on the board, most of them around age sixty, believed this young lawyer might have been too well-prepared. On the 500-mile trip to Austin, Abbie had done most of the driving while Wales read statutes to prepare for his first meeting. He uncovered some details that had escaped his older and more experienced colleagues.

The meeting was called to order, and the agenda was placed before them. Wales hadn't even seen it yet. Normally, agendas were mailed weeks ahead of time, but, of course, he had not been on the board weeks before.

The first item was to award a contract to construct a multi-million dollar building on campus. Wales heard the chairman ask for a motion to approve the construction. A motion was made and seconded, then it was time for a rubber-stamp vote.

"And I said, 'Excuse me, please,'" Wales said. 'I was reading the statutes on the drive down here, and a motion like this must be in writing.' And you could hear the university attorney right away, sort of going, 'What in the hell is this guy talking about?'"

A recess was called, and lawyers huddled. After a break, the regents reconvened.

"They said, 'Regent Madden is exactly right, and we've got to prepare a written approval. We'll do this now if you'll pass on this for a moment,'" Wales said. "People are now looking over at me, going, 'Who is this guy?'"

Ultimately, another motion, this one in writing, was made, and it was approved on a vote. At the next recess, the regents made a point to ask Wales again where he was from and what he did exactly.

"That was fun," he said, "but I didn't rub it in. But from that point on, it was, 'Wales, what do you think?' Instant credibility."

Wales would serve for six years as a UT regent, from 1959 to 1965. He went off the board at the ripe old age of thirty-eight. As he looks back on his life of service, it seems like he was always challenged by age.

University of Texas Board of Regents

"If I look back, age was often an issue in my doing things. Seems to me like I was always appointed to something challenging as a student, elected student body president, and put on a number of committees and immediately became chairman of a number of them," he said. "So I really was used to stepping into situations where you had to have your own smarts and ingenious personality to get things done. It didn't seem hard for me to do it."

Three years into his term as a regent, Wales was asked to be a member of the board of trustees of Trinity University, the prestigious private institution in San Antonio. Trinity was under the umbrella of the Presbyterian church, which is Wales' choice of faith. He soon discovered an unhealthy control of the board that could be hurting the church.

"I could see a clannish control by some board members," he said. "I didn't think the church could progress, let alone survive, with the membership so zealous in holding control."

One of the issues Wales pushed was to open Trinity to students of all denominations in order to broaden the reach for quality students.

"It had been quote, run by several families, close quote, but I could see the credence afforded those family members on the board, and they in turn could see me ready to get after them," he said.

It was as a UT regent that Wales first became friends with one of the true icons of the university, head football coach Darrell Royal. The native of Hollis, Oklahoma, came to Texas in 1957, two years before Wales became a regent. Royal was just three years older than Wales, and the two of them hit it off immediately.

"The only thing that exceeded his ability was his integrity," Wales said. "I marveled at the way he would face an adverse situation and stick right to the truth."

Following the national championship season in 1963, Wales accompanied Royal to New York. The Longhorns had been 11-0, defeating Roger Staubach and Navy in the 1964 Cotton Bowl, and they were awarded the MacArthur Bowl Trophy. The trophy was an anonymous gift in honor of General Douglas MacArthur, a founder of the National Football Foundation. Beginning in 1959, the trophy was awarded annually by the National Football Foundation to the national college champions.

A banquet was held at the Waldorf-Astoria Hotel in New York City, and Wales and Royal attended the gala on behalf of the Longhorns. The Waldorf was also where General Douglas MacArthur lived.

"The weather was so bad that no other regent but me could get there," said Wales, "because I sure wasn't the toughest cow on the board. We were all there for the banquet. We heard how MacArthur wanted to meet Coach Royal. I don't ever remember him asking to meet me."

Royal insisted that Madden was included in his conversation with the General, who had always been quite a football fan. MacArthur had been a student trainer for the football team when he was at West Point.

"What a gentleman he was, and I was surprised how much he knew about Texas football," Wales said. "He couldn't remember specific games, but he could remember critical plays from that season. General MacArthur couldn't have been more polite and receptive, and 'sure glad to have you up here.'"

While the three were together, a photographer for the Associated Press took some photos of MacArthur, Royal, and Madden that would be circulated in newspapers across the country the next day. The framed photo is in Wales' office.

1963 Darrell Royal, General MacArthur and WM

"It was like, 'Who's that guy?'" Wales said of the least famous of the three. "I think the original caption was, 'General Douglas MacArthur, Coach Darrell Royal, and friend.'"

That "friend" became better acquainted with Royal than just watching him on the sidelines or at university functions. Royal stayed with Wales when on recruiting trips to the Panhandle or any other occasion that brought him to the Amarillo area. Wales had a glimpse of Royal that few others had.

Wales would meet Royal at the airport and often chauffeured him to meet a prospective athlete being recruited by Texas. During one trip, they went to visit a family in Amarillo.

"It was kinda cute," Wales said. "There must have been four members of the family there. As we were going into the door, there was kind of a bristle on the part of the grandmother. She said, 'Welcome, Coach Royal, and what's *your* name and why are *you* here?' She didn't exactly say that, but that's what she meant.

"We came in and sat down, and by the time our rears had hit the seat she was telling us what little Jack had been offered last week. The coach from SMU on his visit said he [little Jack] could be the starting quarterback his freshman year. You know that was BS and wasn't going to happen, but that's what she told us.

"Coach Royal, being his usual honest self, said, 'Ma'am, I strongly suggest that you advise your grandson to accept the offer made by SMU because I'm not making any offer now. Thank you for your attention,' and we got up and left."

On another occasion, Royal was staying overnight with the Maddens when a reporter tracked him down by phone. The father of a recruit had made an allegation that Royal had made an improper and illegal offer to his son. The reporter was wanting to get Royal's side of the story and his response.

"That's a damn lie!" he said.

Wales tried to get his friend to calm down. Royal hung up the phone and began to pace around the den.

"He said, 'I'm going to call the SOB [the father].'

"I said, 'It's ten at night. If you still feel the same way in the morning, then okay, but let's sleep on it.'"

Royal went to the guest bedroom, and they both got up early the next morning. Wales had already fixed the coffee.

"I said, 'How you doing?'" Wales said.

"He said, 'I'm not doing too good. I'm going to call the SOB right now.' Oh, boy, at least he was consistent."

During his time as head coach from 1957-1976, Royal won three national titles, eleven Southwest Conference championships, and was 167-47-5. Despite his ongoing success, he had his rocky times with supporters and powerful men.

It was a little rough during the 1976 season when injuries were a factor in a 5-5-1 season. As the season was winding down, powerful regent Frank Erwin and former Governor Allan Shivers supported a private move to fire Royal. Erwin and Shivers were both friends of Wales, but he sided with his friend Royal in this matter.

"I called Frank and said, 'I assume you're not going to take any action about firing the head coach,'" Wales said. "He said that no, they were going to fire him. It just went all over me.

"I said, 'Listen, I'm going to get Coach Royal now, and we're going to call a press conference for seven this evening. We are going to go into the background of you all and the threats you've made against Darrell.' It was kind of 'Whoa, whoa, whoa.'

"I said, 'No, seven o'clock.' I talked to them again later in the day, and they told me that they would respect, not *expect*, but *respect*, Coach Royal's resignation. We would agree he would remain as athletics director, and it worked out just like that. I thought if I didn't step out in that kind of deal, what would have happened to Coach Royal?"

Royal became athletics director and served in that capacity until 1980. The two remained friends until Royal became incapacitated by Alzheimer's disease. Royal died in November 2012 at age eighty-eight.

In the 1970s, Wales became a member of the UT Men's Athletic Council. Women's athletics were about to take a large leap during that time. Just as he had done by appointing blacks to committees when he was student body president, Wales worked to get more female representation on the council.

Soon after leaving the council in 1981, Wales tackled a pet peeve that he wanted changed. It was the attorney and college football fan coming out of him.

Unlike in the NFL, when a college team was penalized, the person who committed the penalty was not identified by jersey number. Wales believed the player should be identified. He took up a cause that would last for years, first with the Southwest Conference, then later with the NCAA.

Over the years he spelled out his reasoning in letters to UT Athletics Council Chairman Dr. L.O. Morgan, UT Athletic Director DeLoss Dodds, Southwest Conference Commissioner Fred Jacoby, and Big 12 Commissioner Steve Hatchell, as well as to college coaches, NCAA committee members, and numerous members of the media.

He believed (1) that the guilty party should be made known to the fans; if basketball players had to raise a hand when committing a foul, why should football players be anonymous? (2) that if a player knew he would be identified, he might be less inclined to commit a penalty; and (3) that identifying the player by number would also make officials more accountable, since they would be calling out specific individuals.

"I think it's time we move to correct this situation," Wales wrote numerous times, "and I hope the University of Texas will take the lead in accomplishing the change."

It took years of quiet persistence. It wasn't really a crusade, but Wales kept the matter in the forefront of decision-makers.

"I had been bitching about that for a long, long time," he said. "That's the only activity in human life where you're not entitled to know your accuser. Why exempt some guy who clipped another and cost him fifteen yards?"

The Southwest Conference athletic directors approved the measure in 1988; however, it wasn't until the 2004 season that the NCAA enacted the measure for all games. Nick Saban, who had won five national titles at Alabama and LSU, backed the identification rule.

Saban, who was on the rules committee, told *USA Today* in 2003, "It takes us three plays with the guys running up and down the sideline to say, 'Who was the hold on?' You're just giving information to the fans. I don't think we're doing it to embarrass the players."

For Wales, it was worth all the effort.

"A man called me and told me I had finally got it done," he said, "and in so many words said he was so damn glad that all of this was behind me because he got so tired of me and others staying after it. Someone said, 'If we would have known what you were like, we would have approved it years ago.' It was just persistence."

Wales has given a lifetime of service to his alma mater. It's a long list: Committee of 75, Board of Regents, nearly fifty years as a member of the Law School Foundation Board, Athletics Council, Chairman of the Development Board, President of the Ex-Students' Association, nearly thirty years as a member of the Littlefield Society, chairman and member of the Chancellor's Council. There's probably more.

In 2002, Wales was honored by UT with the Santa Rita Award. He had been honored by Texas on several occasions, including a Distinguished Alumnus award in 1979, but the Santa Rita is the highest recognition the university can give to an alumnus who demonstrates his commitment to UT and to higher education.

1979 UT Distinguished Alumnus Award
L-R: Pat Babb, WM, George Morris, Bob Bauman and BR Barfield

"At that time, only sixteen had been awarded in 100 years," Wales said. "It got to be a little bit embarrassing because we have so many graduates now who are big shots around the world, and you have one award like this? Come on."

Madden accepts UT award

AUSTIN (AP) – Amarillo attorney Wales H. Madden Jr. accepted the University of Texas System's highest honor Wednesday night and exhorted those in the audience to get the Legislature's attention to help with financial problems facing the system.

He said the most important thing for the university now is its relationship with the governor and the Legislature.

Madden used an analogy of planet alignment and compared the Legislature to Jupiter when it passes behind the sun and isn't visible to those on Earth.

"If you take from this wonderful occasion tonight one quest only let it be this: contact your friends on Jupiter, bring them back to sight and remind them that we need their help," he said.

Madden, 75, received the Santa Rita Award for extraordinary contributions to the UT System and higher education in Texas. He is the 17th person to receive the honor.

"The large footprints leading to this most respected award caused me to wonder how my feet would ever fit," he said "No doubt previous recipients also questioned their having been accepted.

"Now please understand me, although those questions do plague me, I'm not suggesting that there be a recount."

Madden served on the UT board of regents from 1959 to 1965.

He was a member of the Texas Higher Education Coordinating Board from 1969 to 1973 and has participated in several statewide education planning groups, including the Governor's Committee on Public School Education from 1966 to 1969 and the State's Select Committee on Higher Education from 1985 to 1987.

"Wales has done just about everything that could be done to advance the cause of higher education in the University of Texas System and it's component institutions," Peter Flawn, former president of the university, said Wednesday night.

Charles Miller, chairman of the UT board of regents, said previously that Madden "has served the UT system in numerous capacities with the greatest distinction for more than 50 years. Texas higher education has no more loyal friend and no more visionary supporter."

Source: *Amarillo Globe-News*

At the presentation of the Santa Rita at the Four Seasons Hotel in Austin in October 2002, just about a half century after Wales had left UT, former president Peter Flawn closed his remarks with this:

"In this digital age, in evaluating contributions, superlatives such as 'excellent,' 'superior,' or 'outstanding' are not given the weight of numbers, and one is pressed to look at the 'metrics.' What are Wales' 'metrics'?

"If the value of the university endowments created during Wales' leadership of the Centennial Commission, the Development Board, and the 'We're Texas' campaign are added to the value of his time calculated at the hourly rate charged by an attorney for, say, five hours a week for fifty years, the resulting number is followed by eight zeroes! And that does not include a number of those intangibles of wit, humor, and good advice. Good metrics, Wales."

AN AFFAIR WITH THE GREAT OUTDOORS

Wales' love of majestic mountains, with cold streams in the high country and trails that lead to who knows where, is not lifelong. Not quite. He didn't take to the great outdoors until he was at least five or six years old.

1933 Ninny and the kids, Almont, CO

When he was a small boy, Wales traveled with his parents from Amarillo to Gunnison, Colorado. His heart beat faster when he felt the chilly air around Almont, Colorado, which foretold the fresh and different world he was entering. Almont was a small village with just a few cabins. A large stream ran right through town with two smaller streams nearby, feeding into the larger one.

Wales Sr. and WM with trout

The family stayed at a lodge owned by the Britton family. Wales had a BB gun and was an excellent shot even though he had barely started to school. Wales' first paying job may have been with the Brittons. He chopped wood for them, and an agreement was reached that he would be paid a nickel for every blackbird he shot.

"They had to quit that because I was such a good shot that I was flooding them with birds," Wales said.

As he grew older, he acquired a skill which would become a lifelong passion-fly fishing. Not only was his father, Wales, Sr., an excellent fisherman, but there were also two Spanish-American War veterans living in the Almont vicinity who took it upon themselves to teach young Wales the art of fly fishing, educating him annually for about five years.

"Smith and Campbell were their names, that's all I ever knew them by," Wales said. "They adopted me to teach me how to fish. It was a tremendous compliment. They immediately told me I could become a great trout fisherman because I could cast the fly correctly, I could wade into the streams, and I was not afraid. They would walk me along the bank and show me what to look for when I was trying to catch a trout," he said. "There were some places along the stream where you fish for three hours and not even get a strike. Others, first cast, get a strike."

The Maddens would head to Colorado for two weeks every summer. It was the perfect getaway to take his father's mind off the legal practice back in Amarillo, and his mother enjoyed the time there as well.

As Wales approached his teenage years, he wanted to work on the ranch of his uncle, H.M. Kennedy, in the New Mexico mountains. He had to choose—work in New Mexico or go fly fishing in Colorado? Work, and the prospect of some money, won out.

Wales first learned to ride a horse in the mountains of New Mexico. It was serious riding that included roping and corralling cattle, for which he was paid the handsome salary of ten dollars a month.

"And I wasn't worth it," he said. "No one tried any harder. It was fun and work."

His uncle, a former Texas Ranger and an experienced cowboy, was injured at the time and was unable to rope. Wales and another nephew worked the cattle. The long hours, the sunshine and fresh air, being on horseback—all of that appealed to Wales.

"I could work honestly from sunup to sundown," he said. "I just loved it."

Neighbors to the north would join the Kennedy crew to help round up fifty to eighty head of cattle. In turn, Kennedy's crew would return the favor, but they would be rounding up sheep instead of cattle.

Me and R.W on Doc's ranch 1939

1939 working on Doc's ranch in NM

"They have a mind of their own, and it's not much of a mind," Wales said. "We would round up those sheep on horse and on foot. We'd drag them out of the flock and bring them over to where you'd cut their tails off and castrate the males.

"I would learn that the guy who caught the sheep was going to get squirted in the face with blood. That kept happening to me. It really made me mad. It seemed like everyone, including my uncle, was putting me out as the guy to get blood squirted in my face by those dad gum sheep. It was part of growing up. I decided I didn't want to be in the sheep business."

Early on that may have confirmed Wales' desire to be a lawyer, not a shepherd; to seek out a library, not a corral. Now, if he could have made a living as a fly fisherman, that would be a different story. In that case, he may have never opened a law book.

"I love the thrill of wading and sometimes falling and getting water in your waders," he said. "Yet, spotting a pond that you knew, if you did it right, that pond would house up to twelve- and fourteen-inch rainbow trout. Not every stream was like that, but the ones I had a chance to fish were.

"It was syncing up and properly casting that first fly, and seeing that fish hit the fly and then backing up or going forward, wherever the fish went, you just followed that fish. The whole thing is a thrill, just the challenge of it."

While Wales traveled extensively in his life, he usually kept to a familiar routine when choosing places to fly fish. He fished with his old friends on the streams and lakes south of Creed, Colorado and with the family on the ranch near the Colorado/Wyoming border.

1963 "Stag Trip" to Stream's Lake, CO

"Fishing," he said, "was a sport for me."

Hiking was a close second to his passion for fishing. For Wales, the two pastimes went hand in hand. In one, he stalked fish; in the other, he stalked beauty. In both, he would patiently await the rewards, either pulling in the twelve-inch trout or arriving at the top of a 14,000-foot mountain in the Rockies.

When Wales was in high school, he began hiking and mountain climbing not far from his backyard in his beloved Palo Duro Canyon. He has always been drawn to the rugged canyon between Amarillo and Canyon.

"It was just so much fun and such a beautiful thing for me to be in some place in that canyon," he said. "When I was in the Navy, I would see people from Texas, and most had never heard of Palo Duro Canyon. I thought, 'Golly, I want to show folks that place.' And I really did make an effort to the extent that my situation would permit me to do it."

2006 hiking Palo Duro Canyon State Park

In addition to Palo Duro Canyon, some of Wales' favorite hiking places have been in the hills of Central Texas, in and around the canyons and wooded areas near Austin. In Colorado, there are approximately fifty-four 14,000-foot peaks, and Wales has climbed roughly forty-five of them. In New Mexico, he's climbed the three highest mountains in the state, all of them located southwest of Raton.

Climbing and hiking was sometimes a solo pursuit for Wales, but often it was a shared experience. Wales has been the guide with others being faithful followers, as if they had a choice.

"I've taken good friends who would go with me anywhere I was going to hike," he said. "I kind of got a reputation of being reliable and not getting people into trouble. I didn't ever knowingly get someone on top of a mountain that they were tired and couldn't get off of. But I was-and still am for my age-in good shape."

Unlike with fly fishing, Wales has not restricted his climbing to the Rockies, or even to the United States. Wales has climbed the highest mountains in the British Isles, most of them around 4,000 feet, including the highest of them all in Scotland. And as names go, Wales has scaled the highest peak in Wales. He also has climbed some of the French Alps, believing he has reached the top of the three highest peaks.

Wales estimated that sixty percent of his hikes and climbs were solo efforts. Although he liked nothing better than to take several friends or family members with him, sometimes schedules did not permit. At other times he found a quiet journey refreshing and relaxing. Still, he was often the Pied Piper of the Colorado peaks.

"I found, immodestly, let's say in Vail," he said, "the word would leak out that here's that nut from Amarillo, but he's a good guy, and if you want to climb, he'll get you there. It really was that. I had more people contact me to guide them going up the mountain than I could take care of.

"I would not let the pupil push the teacher around because it would get the pupil in trouble and the teacher sued. I was careful about that."

It was through a climbing connection that Wales earned a featured spot in the July 4 Veterans' Parade in Vail. He and a friend became acquainted with a woman from Vail, Pat Hammond, who climbed at least a dozen mountains with them. Pat discovered that Wales had been in the Navy at the end of World War II, which was about the same she met her future Navy husband and moved with him to Colorado. About five years ago she organized the annual parade in Vail.

"I watch the parade and it goes right by our house, and it's gorgeous," he said. "It's just so fascinating, the old-timey bands and the people marching. I said, 'Gee, I'm impressed with all these veterans, and she said, 'Were you actually in the war?' I said, 'Sure was. I was in the Pacific.' She said, 'You're going to be in the head Jeep and throw candy to the kids.' I've done that several times, and now I'm the oldest veteran from World War II able to ride or walk-the oldest one!"

Wales passed on his love and skill of hiking first to his children, Wales III and Tawney, and later to his grandchildren. He said that at first his children did not see the fascination in it, but they came around. So did his grandchildren, especially his oldest grandson, Mac Macfarlan.

Hamilton, Mac and WM   Mac, Wales IV, Hamilton and Callie

"Mac is the greatest hiker," said his grandfather. "Mac has hiked almost half the Continental Divide. He has hiked and camped by himself, and he got all of that from me. He is still an avid and enthusiastic hiker. His sister (Callie) not that entirely, but those two kids, I'm telling you, they are something.

"They'll say, 'Hey, Pap-Paw,' guess what I saw today?' They will tell me what kind of animal they saw. Inadvertently, I have reared a pack of these four, and maybe more, young kids who just love the outdoors. I'm proud of that."

As the summer of 2016 rolls around, Wales is no longer able to hike and climb like he did for nearly seventy years, but the memories remain. The lure and challenge of the canyons around Amarillo that he faced and loved as a teenager never left, decade after decade. Like fly fishing, hiking is a part of who Wales is.

"It's the challenge of knowing that few people are able to do it," he said. "I can't tell you the feeling I have when I get on the peak of a 14,500-foot mountain and sit there and just say, 'Thank you, God. Thank you for letting me get up here. I didn't fall. I didn't hurt myself. These people didn't get hurt, and what a beautiful, beautiful world you have.'

"That's not baloney with me. I get tingling in my arms about that. Hiking has been a vital part of my life. The thrill of that 14,500-foot peak and you able to get up there, and say, 'OK, world here I am.' That's hard to beat."

WM and Tigi-made it to the top

WM and Tigi at the top again

WM celebrates his 80ᵗʰ on Mount Bross, (14,184' ASL) with Willie and Dean

PRESTIGE AND POLITICAL PALS

Wales Madden has never been far from political races, beginning with his days at the University of Texas and continuing well into the twenty-first century. It was a natural fit. Friends sought his help, and Wales had a passion for effective government and for helping to put those he admired into elected positions in order for effective government to work. That, and he just had a hard time saying no.

When political friends asked for his time, his service, or his money, Wales was more than willing to oblige. It began with painting bare feet on the UT sidewalks for student body president Barefoot Sanders in the early 1950s and continued through helping George W. Bush in his race for the White House more than fifty years later. In between, he became friends with former presidents Lyndon Johnson, George H.W. Bush, and George W. Bush and with former governor John Connally, as well as numerous other federal, state, and local politicians.

Other than his time as Interfraternity Council president and later student body president at Texas, Wales never entered the campaign. Helped? Oh, yes. Served? That too. Although he was asked many times to be a candidate, he refrained.

"I had a bunch of chances," he said.

It wasn't that he didn't think he would win or didn't want to serve. Quite the contrary. Wales thought he could win, but deep down he believed Abbie and his children didn't want him to run for public office. Wales III told his dad he would probably be in and out of fights on almost a daily basis, defending his dad's honor.

In the mid-1960s Congressman Walter Rogers called Wales, who had been a big supporter, to tell him that in a few days he would announce he would not run for re-election. Rogers broached the idea that if his friend would then announce his candidacy, he would throw his support to Wales.

"I said, 'Oh, Walter, let me call some people,'" Wales said. "This sounds braggadocios, but I knew several congressmen, not only in Texas, but elsewhere. I called between six and eight over the weekend, and all took the call."

Wales laid it out to them. Rogers was likely not going to run again and wanted Wales to seek the post. Since he thought he could win, Wales wanted to know what life would be like for him, even in the first five days of office.

"I had my kids there with Abbie listening on the speaker phone," he said. "They [the congressmen] would go through it all, and it sounded God-awful. Just constant calls and meetings and not getting home until late. Some of them couldn't afford to bring their family up there. They had to leave them in Tennessee or wherever they were. They didn't get to see them except on weekends and holidays.

"I could just see my kids going, 'Oooooh, no.' I was pretty well convinced, before I needed to call any more, that I loved my children and my family more than I loved the opportunity to serve."

Wales called Rogers back, telling him to do what he planned to do, but he was not going to announce for Congress. Instead, Bob Price of Pampa won the seat. It was a seat Wales likely could have had, but he had no regrets. Wales still managed the fulfillment of political campaigning and service to others by helping behind the scenes and by helping and knowing the most powerful men in the world.

The first was a fellow Texan, Lyndon Johnson. Johnson was a U.S. senator who had aspirations to run for the presidency in 1960. The two had a mutual friend, Lloyd Hand. Hand had been a year ahead of Wales at Texas and preceded him as student body president.

Hand, who had become influential in the business world, persuaded Johnson to meet Wales and develop a friendship because Wales' help could be crucial. Wales wasn't even sure he could support Johnson, but he was persuaded to take a leave of absence from Shamrock on two different occasions to help with Johnson's campaign.

"He and I did have a very cordial relationship," Wales said, "because I was interested in some of the really good things he wanted to do for the country. That made me a liberal in the eyes of some, but not in my eyes."

Wales' assignment was to go to Delaware, of all places. He was given a list of about ten of the state's congressmen with their addresses and phone numbers. He was tasked with persuading them to vote for Johnson.

"I'll be durned if I didn't get every one of those guys to agree," he said. "They said, 'Yeah, we'll support Lyndon.' Of course, those things filter out in a campaign organization. All of a sudden, this no-name from Amarillo, Texas, is a real stud. That rolls into the next occasion."

While Wales was in Delaware, he received an additional assignment he knew nothing about. A stevedore on the docks in an adjacent state needed some persuasion to support LBJ as well.

"It was night, and he was loading stuff on the ship," Wales said. "I was walking, kinda helping, kicking along and saying, 'Well, Mr. Johnson sure is a great man and is someone you can be proud of.' This guy said, 'Oh, s—, I don't want to be proud of anybody. I want to get paid.' I said, 'Well, I'm not authorized to pay you,' and I was thinking I better get out of there right now."

At the 1960 Democratic convention in Los Angeles, both Wales and Jerry Johnson, a longtime Amarillo attorney and Democratic supporter, were in attendance. Jerry was helping the Johnson campaign, too, but only Wales had a pass for the convention.

"I said, 'Jerry, come on, I'll get you in. Let's go.' He said, 'How you going to do it?' I said, 'It will be a quick hand pass. You stand right behind me and get ready to receive this because it's coming right back to you.' They didn't have photographs on them back then.

"So I get up there, and I hear, 'Hey, boys, where are y'all from?' I give out a big twang, 'I'm from Amarillo, Texas,' and Jerry's right behind me. He grabbed the pass, and I said to let us go through. They asked where his pass was, and he showed them my pass, and we got in."

Wales liked Lyndon Johnson, although his acceptance of some of LBJ's political positions was marginal.

"Being with him and his wife and two other couples on his ranch was a real treat," he said. "Abbie and I were always impressed by how nice he was to us when we went to his ranch. He would treat us like royalty. Abbie and Mrs. Johnson were such pure Christian-believing people and so delightful. So I think the president thought that anyone who had such a fine person for a wife must be OK. I mean, really."

LBJ and friends

When Wales was at the Johnson ranch, or later at the White House talking with the Bushes, he couldn't help but reflect on how a young boy from Amarillo, the son of a lawyer, could be in the company of some of the greatest Americans in modern history.

"I would think, 'How the hell did I get here? What makes me different?'" he said. "But all my life, occasions like that have arisen, and I'd end up being with the big shots and wondering what I'm doing around this guy."

That may have never been more true than on one occasion when Wales was in Washington on business. He had called the president on more than one occasion when he was in D. C.

"Usually I'd stay in a hotel that was walking distance from the White House," he said. "And the president would say, 'Wales, come over here.'"

On this occasion he decided, on a lark, to drop in at the White House to say "hello" to Johnson. Security was much different in the 1960s. Wales was ushered into the White House. Johnson was standing out in the Rose Garden with the U.S. ambassador to the United Nations and the attorney general.

"Here I am, just standing there," Wales said. "He said, 'Fellas, I got to take my friend inside. I've got some people I want him to meet.'"

So Wales followed President Johnson into the cabinet room where the full cabinet was about to meet. They were among the most powerful people in the country.

"There is the entire cabinet sitting around the big table," Wales said. "The president said, 'Fellas, I've got someone I want you to meet. He's one of my best friends. He's Wales Madden from Amarillo, Texas, and he's president of the Amarillo Chamber of Commerce.' That's a true story. Don't you know they were impressed by that?"

Banquet Guest

Former Gov. Allan Shivers, now president of the U.S. Chamber of Commerce, left, chats with Wales Madden incoming president of the Amarillo Chamber of Commerce. Shivers was guest speaker at the annual Amarillo chamber banquet Monday night.

Former Governor Allan Shivers and WM
Source: *Amarillo Globe-News*

Neither George H.W. Bush nor his son invited him into the cabinet room when they were president, but Wales did develop a relationship with them, especially the elder Bush.

"The Bushes were wonderful leaders for our country. They were actually never given enough credit for the sincerity they brought to that office," Wales said. "George W.'s father was very generous in what he wanted me to do by serving in part of the government."

Bush, Sr., and Wales were sitting in the Braniff lounge at the Dallas airport in the 1980s. Bush was pondering running for president, and Wales had been following many of his public statements.

"I said, 'Mr. Bush, if you ever do decide to run, count me in.' I think it was the next day he was going to Houston, and I was going to Amarillo. The phone rang, and there he was, 'OK, Wales, let me tell you what I want you to do.' He put me on a committee."

Wales took Abbie to the 1988 Republican convention where Bush was nominated as president. Bush knew of Wales' interest in education, and later he made him chairman of the Board for International Food and Agricultural Development and Economic Cooperation ("BIFADEC"). The committee was composed of four university presidents, a Congressman, and Wales.

President and Mrs. George H.W. Bush and the Maddens

"I quickly dug into it and thought it was a hoax," he said. "This committee exists under the guise of making educational recommendations about agricultural matters and other things in foreign countries. These folks would conduct a hearing on raising corn in central Africa. We didn't have any business doing that."

The paid committee staff was rather large, so Wales waited before he made his statements to make sure he was correct about the foolishness of the committee's existence. After studying the minutes of previous meetings, Wales was certain there were some questionable activities perpetrated by a congressman on the committee. The congressman had a group in Washington that he could control and use to travel to exotic places like Africa. Wales believed it was a guise, ineffective and too expensive.

"I let it drag out for a while, and then I got in touch with President Bush," he said. "I said this is what's happening. He asked me what I thought we should do. I said I'll make a report at the next meeting, and then you should do what you think.

WM and President Bush at the White House

"He said, 'By God, if we don't need it, we won't keep it.' And that's what happened. And then they [committee members] got mad at me right away, thinking they could push me into changing in the course of this."

Bush also asked Wales to chair another committee that interviewed quality candidates from the western part of the U.S. to be considered for federal government assignments. Most were governors or recent governors who wanted to go into a training program. Hearings were held in Dallas for the committee to interview the candidates. The theory was to develop qualified people who would serve and eventually end up in elected office.

"That committee was helpful, but BIFADEC was a ruse," Wales said. "That just shows you a person like Bush can come in and, 'damn the torpedoes,' get rid of unnecessary expenditures."

George H.W. Bush after a humorous introduction

Wales became acquainted with George W. Bush in the 1990s, when he was Texas governor. Bush was a biker, and Wales was a jogger. Most of their conversations took place on the bike trails.

Abbie, George W. and WM

"We would visit about innocuous things, but just keep up with each other," he said. "But he really went out of his way to make me feel a part of the group. He wanted me to be a chairman of one of his committees, and I told him that wasn't fair to him.

"He needed to get out with a younger, more virile group of people. He thought that was a good idea and ended up putting my son [Wales III] on one."

Wales worked on several campaigns for U.S. senators, including John Tower, Phil Gramm, and Kay Bailey Hutchison.

"Phil Gramm was tops," Wales said. "He was not anyone's person. He wanted to change the way we put people in public office in the judiciary."

Gramm called Wales, asking for his help in this matter.

Senator Phil and Wendy Gramm

"He told me we have to get away from how we are putting federal judges into office. I said, 'OK, I'll do it.' I devised an idea of a committee not to exceed twelve lawyers or former lawyers and let it be known they would choose only recommendations from their list of people. As people wanted to be considered, [they would] write a letter [of application] to this committee. And that's where we started.

"At first, people were reluctant. They thought we were just hand maidens of Senator Gramm, but we were not. So we had this committee, the Senatorial Selection Committee. I wrote the rules of the committee."

The committee culled about sixty applicants down to the ten that it would interview. The intention was to recommend three applicants to Gramm.

"We were not hidden in secrecy," he said, "but we observed someone that didn't want a boss knowing they were interviewing. We did this right up to his [Gramm] leaving office."

Of all the governors Wales knew, John Connally might have been his favorite. In 1980 Wales worked on Connally's presidential campaign until he dropped out. "I thought John Connally was ideal to be in public office," he said.

On March 30, 1981, Wales was in Washington to meet with Connally. Although Wales was not well acquainted with Ronald Reagan, he was a friend of Reagan's press secretary, James Brady. Brady had been Connally's chief of staff in 1979 and 1980. He and Wales became friends during the Connally campaign.

James Baker, Abbie, WM and President Reagan

Reagan had just spoken to a group at the Washington Hilton and was returning to the White House when several shots were fired just as he was entering the presidential limousine. Wales was standing in the crowd mostly out of curiosity, but also to wave to Brady and possibly shake Reagan's hand.

"He [Brady] asked me to come by and maybe meet the president," he said. "I could not quite see the president, but I could see my friend falling. He was also hit, but there was a lot of chaos. The police and Secret Service were moving around rapidly. From that point on, I was more worried about Brady who was still on the sidewalk, but alive."

Brady lived until 2014, but his wounds left him debilitated the rest of his life.

From the Johnson ranch to the attempted assassination of a president, Wales found himself in some unique and historic places due to his political connections.

To Alma Faye and Wales Madden
With appreciation and best wishes.

9-22-72

Richard Nixon

Peter Flawn, WM, John Connally

To Walter Madden
With best wishes   JUNE 29, 1983
                                    WHITE HOUSE MEETING

Ronald Reagan

Senator John Cornyn and Karl Rove

A FRIEND NAMED BOONE

By the time Boone Pickens made his way to Amarillo, Wales Madden was about ready to leave; however, the two events were unrelated.

Boone's dad Thomas was an oil landman, and when the Oklahoma oil boom played out, he moved his family to Amarillo. The year was 1944. Boone was sixteen and entered Amarillo High as a junior that fall.

Wales, a senior, was among several students who were graduating early in 1945 in order to serve their country in World War II. Boone, Pat Babb, Sonny Morris, and Wales became friends in the short period before Wales and Pat left Amarillo High for induction into the U.S. Navy. There was about a thirty-minute sendoff ceremony for Wales and Pat in front of Amarillo High. Boone was in the crowd of students who were glad to get out of class, if nothing else.

"The principal got up there and talked about what fine young men they were, that they were going off to save America," Boone said. "I looked at them and thought, 'Gosh almighty, are we down to this? These guys were going to save America?' The next guy on the bus was going to be me, and so we were getting down to the bottom of the barrel."

Wales and Boone would meet again, after Wales had served in the U.S. Navy and left the University of Texas with a law degree, and after Boone had graduated from Oklahoma A&M with a geology degree and began a short stint with Phillips Petroleum.

Wales and Boone, the famous billionaire oil man and financier, rekindled a friendship, both personal and professional, that would sustain them for more than seventy years.

Due to his civic endeavors and leadership role, the name of Madden is known throughout Amarillo, the Texas Panhandle, and the University of Texas, while the name of Pickens has reached beyond, to Wall Street and to the boardrooms of major oil companies, to network news programs and magazine covers. To each other, they are just Wales and Boone.

"He's the brightest, most honest and most driven financial human being I've ever known or will ever know," Wales said. "He is a unique and trustworthy guy. When he passes on, he'll go out that way. If that sounds a little glamorous, it's not. He's very special. We've had quite a life together."

That life together began in the 1950s. Boone began working for Phillips and was transferred to Amarillo from Corpus Christi in 1953. At about that same time, Wales returned to Amarillo with his new bride Abbie and his UT law degree and started working at Shamrock. Boone stayed with Phillips for about another year before striking out on his own.

In 1956 Boone built a house on Harmony, putting him in close proximity to Wales' home on Teckla. High school chums, George Morris and Pat Babb, lived nearby as well. Their children skied together, and the dads and sons hunted and fished together.

The Maynards, Pickens, Babbs, Oles and Maddens before a hunt

When they socialized in one another's homes, the friends would often play "Wildcatter," a homemade board game Boone had invented. The name fit since wildcatting is essentially what he was doing at the time.

The board, made of balsa wood, was in a box about three inches deep. Resembling Hutchinson County, northeast of Amarillo, it was composed of oil fields with either dry wells or gushers. Boone had rigged a stiff piece of wire with a dime welded on the end which players used to "drill" all over the board, searching for oil.

"It was set up similar to Monopoly," Boone said. "That was a fascinating game for a little while."

When Boone divorced wife Lynn in 1971, she threw away not only his 1940 electric train set, but also his Wildcatter game board.

"We're good friends now," he said, "but at the time, I told her I liked to have choked her for doing that."

After tiring of the bureaucracy at Phillips, Boone struck out on his own. In 1956 he and two partners formed Petroleum Exploration, Inc., which became Mesa Petroleum in 1963. When Mesa went public on the American Stock Exchange in 1964, the company had $2 million in assets and no debt. Wales was part of those early drilling partnerships, and he also provided legal advice when Mesa went public. By 1967 Mesa had grown to the point that it was accepted for trading on the "Big Board," the New York Stock Exchange.

September 27, 1967, Mesa's 1ˢᵗ day of trading on the NYSE

As he would do all of his life, Boone was always looking to expand and grow, whether by oil exploration or, in later years, by using his hedge funds in BP Capital Management to invest in traditional energy companies.

Wales became more involved with Mesa, not only from the legal aspect but also as a member of the board of directors. Because of his love of traveling, he often volunteered to visit potential exploration sites for Mesa. He didn't mind going to Norway, Austria, or West Africa, each a little more exotic than a trip he made to Duchesne, Utah, in 1965.

Mesa had a chance to buy Standard Gilsonite property in Utah. The value was not in the property so much as in the shareholders Mesa could obtain. Mesa had only 200 shareholders, while Gilsonite had 1,300.

Wales, Boone, and another associate went to Utah to check out the property. Boone decided to go down into the mine to see what he could see. Wales chose to stay above ground.

Boone said, "I said, 'Wales, are you going to go?' He said, 'No, I'll stay here and tell them what happened.' Wales is smarter than I am, always has been. He stayed above just in case we didn't come back."

Boone and the associate boarded the mine car and slipped into the darkness. For all Wales knew, they were headed 1,000 feet down, but the car went only about twenty feet before it became stuck.

"Wales is getting nervous. I can see him, but he can't see me," Boone said. "Wales is yelling, 'Hey, Boone, Hey, Boone.' I'm right below him, but he doesn't know, and he's getting pretty frantic. He's still yelling, and I don't answer.

"We're still fooling around trying to get the car to move, and so after ten minutes of him yelling and getting louder, I said, 'Hey, Wales, I'm right here.' I thought he was going to faint. We got the car to move back to the surface. We only went twenty feet, and he thought we were 1,000 feet below him."

Mesa bought the property, which wasn't lucrative, but it acquired the stockholders and gained some solid customers, like Halliburton and Dow Chemical. Five years later Mesa sold the property for $100,000 to a company in New Jersey.

"Our mines weren't worth anything," Boone said, "but our customer list was."

Mesa's fame would develop through Boone's acquisitions. The one that set him, his board, and the shareholders on their way was not too far from Amarillo.

In 1968, Boone and Wales targeted the Hugoton Production Company of Garden City, Kansas, for a possible merger. Hugoton owned a substantial portion of the Hugoton Gas Field in southwestern Kansas, the largest gas field in the nation at the time.

When Hugoton management rebuffed Boone's offer, Mesa introduced a hostile tender offer that would give Hugoton shareholders 1.8 shares of Mesa's common stock for every share of Hugoton's. Because Boone was barely forty years old and his company was much the smaller of the two, Hugoton's management and board of directors failed to take him seriously-a big mistake.

Boone and Wales were in New York in discussion with Hugoton which was run by Clark Estates in New York. The Clark attorneys were deposing Boone. When there was a break, Boone and Wales were invited to relax in the office of one of the opposing attorneys. Boone was sitting at the attorney's desk when he noticed something interesting on the desk-proposed deposition questions for Boone.

"Later, this fella started asking Boone questions, and when he was about finished, Boone said, 'Wait, you overlooked one,'" Wales said. "That really ticked him off. He was an imposing attorney."

"I didn't open any drawers, and it was just lying on the desk," Boone said. "They asked me if I looked at them. I wasn't going to lie, and I said, 'Well, I didn't look at them very close.'"

In 1969 Mesa acquired nearly one-third of Hugoton's shares, with the stockholders of both companies approving the merger in April. Hugoton assets gave Mesa the leverage it needed to expand its business and to complete bigger deals.

"The guy is smart," Boone said of Wales. "He established that pretty quick. He had good ideas and gave a great amount of good advice at the right time. I didn't take all of it, but more than he thought I did."

Over the years, Mesa opened offices in Calgary, Houston, Midland, and Denver. In one of his most profitable ventures, Boone invested $35,000 in drilling sites in Canada, sinking the money from those sites into new wells. In 1979 he sold his entire Canadian operation to another oil company for $600 million. By 1981, Mesa was one of the largest independent oil producers in the world.

"The company was moving along pretty good and Wales was in on all that," he said. "We traveled to New York a lot together in working with investment bankers and lawyers. By the seventies, we had found a lot of oil and gas, but now we're running out of places to drill, and it's becoming tougher and tougher to find conventional oil and gas reserves."

That's about the time that Boone famously told his board, "It's cheaper to drill on the New York Stock Exchange."

The 1980s ushered in a period when Boone Pickens and Mesa rocketed to rock star status. Boone persuaded the board to use Mesa money to buy stock in publicly held oil companies which he had determined to be either undervalued or badly mismanaged. Mesa's brazen attempted takeovers of such industry giants as Gulf, Phillips, Cities Service, and Unocal landed Boone on the covers of *Time* and *Fortune* magazines.

Mesa never acquired those companies but, in effect, brought them to their knees, often forcing a merger with other companies in order to keep Mesa at bay. As he had promised, Boone increased the value of Mesa stock, reaping millions for stockholders and millions for Mesa. From 1982 to 1985, it was reported that Mesa made $800 million in the takeover attempts.

The walls of Wales' office suite have a number of nationally syndicated cartoons and magazine covers featuring Boone, along with a signed note that Boone sent his old friend, reminders of those heady times.

"We've never had to apologize for anything," Boone said. "There's a little difference where we started then and where we are today. We're getting too damn old."

In 1987, Mesa was involved in a public spat with *Amarillo Globe-News*, which Boone felt had covered the company and himself unfairly. It was a prolonged squabble. At one point, when editor Jerry Huff left for Arkansas, Mesa draped a large gold banner across the top of Mesa's ten-story building in downtown Amarillo that read, "Goodbye, Jerry."

"There was a little blame on each side," Wales said. "I thought it was an unfair indictment of Boone from the paper, and they made a mistake that caused Boone to react the way he did. Boone grew less and less tolerant, and I blame him for that, but he still constantly sought my advice in those little disputes. Most of his officers wanted to move out of Amarillo. You had that situation, and finally he announced he was leaving Amarillo, but Boone is a tough, kind, and generous person mentally, and used to be physically."

Mesa moved to Dallas in 1989. A few years later one of Boone's gambles-and there were a lifetime of those-blew up. He used Mesa earnings to purchase large natural gas reserves, thinking the price would go up. It never did. In fact, prices declined to debilitating levels. As a result, Mesa became saddled with $1.2 billion in debt. In true Shakespearian irony, the company became the target of a takeover by a former top Mesa executive, David Batchelder of Relational Investors.

Boone blocked Batchelder's attempt by arranging for mega-investor Richard Rainwater of Fort Worth to invest $265 million, essentially giving Rainwater control of Mesa. Then a plan was formed to force Boone out. Just like that, the company that Boone originally formed with $2,500 he had borrowed nearly forty years earlier was out of his hands.

Those who thought Boone would quietly slip away didn't know him. Wales knew his old friend would not do that. Using the same smarts and daring as before, Boone reinvented himself, this time using hedge funds instead of oil.

The following year, he founded BP Capital Management, the letters standing not for British Petroleum, but for—well, that's easy to guess. BP operated two hedge funds, Capital Commodity and Capital Equity, which invested in traditional energy companies. Boone also has been an advocate for alternative energy, including solar and wind energy.

In 2006, BP Capital earned $1 billion and in 2007, $2.7 billion. By 2008, before the stock market took a serious tumble in October,

Boone's wealth was estimated at $4 billion. Although the market crash reduced it, his wealth in 2016 was estimated to be still a little more than $1 billion.

Boone purchased water rights below more than 150,000 acres near Pampa in Roberts County. In 2011 he sold water from the Ogallala Aquifer beneath his land to the Canadian Municipal Water Authority. Boone's Mesa Water and Mesa Water Holding signed a $103 million water deal with Panhandle officials, the largest ever in the history of the area.

Boone hasn't given away all the money he's made, but his philanthropic gifts have made a difference in lives and institutions. He has given away an estimated $800 million, including more than $500 million given to his alma mater, Oklahoma State University. Both the football stadium and the School of Geology bear his name.

To prove that he can appreciate different shades of orange, even burnt orange, Boone donated $100 million to Wales's alma mater, specifically to the University of Texas Southwestern Medical Center.

Although Boone moved from his and Wales' hometown nearly thirty years ago, he has a spectacular ranch home in Roberts County, a get-away where he is able to pursue one of his lifelong passions, bird hunting.

Wales and Boone spent many a leisure hour together outdoors. When they were younger, they skied together. In later years, they joined in each other's favorite pursuits, Wales with Boone's hunting, and Boone with Wales' fly fishing.

Pheasant hunt

"I had to kill all his birds for him," Boone said. "He was a pretty good fisherman, but he never hunted as a boy like I did. He never had that experience, but when he got into it, he liked it. We always had a good time hunting and fishing."

1967 2B Ranch
Boone, Bobby Stillwell, Jerry Walsh and WM

These two warriors and longtime friends are separated by only eight and a half months in age. In May 2016, at eighty-eight years of age, Boone, like his old friend Wales, still keeps a vigorous pace. Boone is able to remember Wales' birthday, September 1, because it falls on the opening day of dove season. They have been loosely tied to each other, off and on, for seventy years. Wales' admiration and respect for Boone has never wavered, and the same can be said for Boone.

Boone said of Wales, "One, I don't like him-I love him. So start there. We've been friends for so long, and, two, we made some money together. We've been in contact in one way or another since he went off to win the war.

"And thank God, he did."

HONORING SYBIL'S WISHES

Don Harrington came to the Texas Panhandle during the Borger oil boom of the 1920s. It wasn't long before he met and eventually married Sybil Buckingham. In the meantime, he became one of the first wealthy oil men in the Panhandle.

The Harringtons felt a need to share their success with the less fortunate. In 1951, the Don and Sybil Harrington Foundation was endowed, followed by Don's creation of the Amarillo Area Foundation, a public philanthropic foundation for the twenty-six counties of the Texas Panhandle. Over the years those institutions have improved the area's quality of life immensely.

On an early April evening in 2016 the crowd at the Amarillo Country Club was a large one. The occasion was the recognition of four Harrington Fellows from the University of Texas, two graduate students and two faculty members.

Also being honored was a man who had roamed the UT campus once upon a time, a man whose impact on the university was approaching sixty-five years, a man without whose efforts the Don D. Harrington Fellows Program at UT likely would not exist.

On this evening, Wales Madden was named an honorary Harrington Fellow for his work to fulfill Sybil Harrington's wishes for a fellowship program to rival the Fulbright and Guggenheim fellowships.

"When we think of the origin of the Donald D. Harrington Fellows program, two names immediately come to mind, obviously Don and Sybil Harrington," Mark Bivins told the gathering. "There is a third person, however, who has played a critical role in not only the founding of the program but also its continued success.

"Both behind the scenes and in the public limelight, this stalwart UT supporter has not only brought the Harrington Fellowship to life but has given his burnt orange blood, sweat, and tears to just about every aspect of our great university. I know the suspense is killing you on just who he is."

Bivins continued, "Sybil was never quite satisfied that she had done enough, and she always wanted to do something more for 'her Don,' as she called her sweet Don Harrington, who passed away in 1974.

"In order for Sybil to fully execute her very small idea of creating a world-class scholarship program that would appeal to students world-wide and be on the level of the Rhodes Scholarship, she needed a little help. This was a job for Wales Madden."

The job was Wales' because of Sybil Harrington's trust in him. Don Harrington died in 1974 after a fall at the Amarillo airport. Sybil called Wales and Avery Rush, wanting them to be independent executors of the estate. Both men said they wanted to help her but didn't feel like they could be executors.

Sybil was impressed with their candidness and filed that way. Ten years later, in 1984, she had an idea for a project with far-reaching impact. She wanted her friend Wales to take her idea and run with it.

Wales said, "This is a whole episode of my life that I take great pride in. She said, 'OK, Willie,' (that's what she called me), 'I want to create an institution to memorialize Don's name. I want people at a great university to know him. Now your job, Willie, is to tell me how to do it and see that it gets done.'"

Wales asked if she had a university in mind. She said Notre Dame was a possibility, as were several Ivy League schools.

"I said, 'That's the quickest way to bury his name that you could find. They wouldn't have the interest that you have in Don. As a result, you would never know what they were going to do.' She said, 'I guess you would want it to go the University of Texas,' and I said, 'I sure would.'"

As soon as Wales left that meeting with Sybil, he excitedly called UT President Bill Cunningham, who in turn contacted Executive Vice President and Provost Gerald Fonken and Vice President Shirley Bird Perry.

"They wanted to come up and visit with Sybil, but she wouldn't visit with them," Wales said. "I said, 'Well, they will bring you to Austin.' She said, 'Oh, God, that's even more horrible.' She really did. I told her that she didn't have to do either one of those. I would do what I could to carry out her wishes."

Wales and Sybil met to discuss the specifics of the fellowship. Early on, Sybil felt it might be focused on the petroleum field with an emphasis on engineering, since that was her late husband's field of study. Ultimately, she changed her mind, concluding that, for the fellowship to be sought internationally, the program should have no limits on academic disciplines.

The fellowship would be funded through the Harrington Foundation, as well as through Sybil's personal finances, with the balance to be designated in a testamentary disposition under her will. She insisted there would be no publicity until after her death.

When UT had received most of her donated funds, Wales made one final effort in 1990 to convince Sybil that she should be recognized for her benevolence while she was alive. He wrote her a letter urging a dinner and reception in her honor. If not that, then a scaled-down social function. If not that, just a simple announcement.

Her written responses on the returned letter: "Ghastly." "Never." "We can skip everything." She ended her letter with this: "And this is how it should be handled, with Mr. Wales Madden, Jr., presiding over dinners, teas, receptions, luncheons, brunches, etc. These are my final words...Hugs & Kisses, Sybil."

Sybil Harrington died in 1998. Soon after, her academic honor to her husband, the Donald D. Harrington Fellows program, was publicly announced. Behind the scenes, Wales had written the creation of the fellowship program with the guidelines provided by Sybil.

Wales spoke at the formal announcement of the Harrington Fellows program in Austin in November 2000. A good portion of his speech that day was an explanation of why Sybil wanted no publicity until after her death.

"She asked, on a number of occasions, that I explain to the president and his associates that she was sorry that she could not come to Austin and how much she appreciated their kindness," Wales said. "She said, 'Just blame it on an old lady who is tired of traveling.'"

But she never tired of providing financially for others, be it charitable giving or, in this instance, supporting elite academic achievement.

Wales told an audience at the formal announcement of the Harrington Fellowship, "A sensitive romanticist would suggest that they were our Lady Guinevere and Sir Lancelot who beckoned us to join them for one glorious moment at Camelot."

The Harrington Fellowship unfolded just as Sybil, Wales, and the University of Texas envisioned. Top graduate students and faculty members not only from the United States but also from overseas applied annually for the one-year fellowship to study at UT.

Faculty members are selected based on their research performance and potential for original contributions to research in fields of great significance globally. Graduate students are named based on their academic records, character, and leadership. It's no stretch to say the Harrington Fellows are among the brightest and most gifted students in the world.

Graduate students and faculty from the world's top universities have been selected. Through 2016, 129 graduate students and sixty-four faculty have been Harrington Fellows. For fourteen years, they have traveled to Wales' hometown of Amarillo for a research symposium.

In 2015-2016, thirty graduate fellows and three faculty fellows were named. They were represented at the symposium in Amarillo by two graduate students and two faculty members. Presentations were made by Heidi Culver of Johns Hopkins in Biomedical Engineering and by Santiago Papini of City University of New York in Clinical Psychology, along with faculty fellows Rastko S. Jakovljevic of the University of Durham, United Kingdom, in Anthropology of Music and Ioulia Kovelman of the University of Michigan in Communication Sciences and Disorders.

As usual, Wales Madden was in the audience. This time he was there not only to see firsthand the true meaning of the Harrington Fellows program but also to be named an honorary Harrington Fellow.

"Wales has been a delight," said Dr. Marv Hackert, interim dean of graduate studies at UT who has been involved with the Harrington Fellows for eleven years. "One of the things I've enjoyed most about my work at UT is with the Harrington and getting to know Wales. He's been shaping the future of UT since he graduated from law school in 1952.

"Wales, when you encouraged Sybil Harrington to establish a fellowship at UT, you created a pathway for the university to innovate that's really hard to measure. I know Mrs. Harrington was pleased that you made the case for your alma mater, and today UT is one of the thirty best research universities in the world, and the Harrington Fellowship has played a big part in that.

"This is our opportunity to say, 'Thank you, Wales.' There are not enough words to express our gratitude to you. But in bestowing this honorary Harrington Fellow, just know, as we say at UT, 'Once a Harrington Fellow, always a Harrington Fellow.'"

With that, Wales was asked to come forward to a standing ovation, and Hackert read the plaque: "Wales Madden, Jr., for his dedication, passion, and leadership in the establishment and advancement of the Donald D. Harrington Fellows program, is hereby named an honorary Harrington Fellow."

In his typical self-deprecating style, Wales said, "I can see Sybil saying, 'What are you going to do next? You're taking credit for this? Sit down, Willie, and shut up,'" and, with that, he did.

In a more serious, reflective moment, when taking in the scope of the outstanding students and faculty who have researched and studied at his alma mater by way of a prestigious fellowship from a friend to honor one of the Texas Panhandle's most benevolent pioneers, Wales couldn't help but feel a sense of satisfaction and reward.

"When I'm gone," he said, "one of the things I will end my life being most proud of is I met everything Sybil wanted in creating the Don Harrington Fellowship."

ABBIE THE ARTIST

Wales thumbed through the pages of *Abbie's Anthology*, the book of some of the most meaningful paintings that Abbie Madden had created. It was a collection of more than 150 paintings compiled by Wales III and his wife Nita. Each page had a special meaning, a memory for Wales. There was no picking his favorite. They were all his favorites, but none more so than her last, "Untitled."

"Let me see what I wrote," Wales said as he read the words printed next to the painting. "The last painting was one of her finest works in progress, typical of the dedication to perfection in producing the painting.

"The artist was not satisfied with the lead cowboy. She was in the process of re-entering the lead and his horse. She smudged them out in order to make them more life-like. The cowboy's legs were poorly proportioned. She partially erased them in the spring of 2012.

"She had almost signed off on the paleness of the sky, the ruggedness of the cliffs exaggerated by the snow, the weariness of the longhorn's leg as it trudged through that deepening snow as the herd struggled further south down the canyon. She wanted the harsh impact of the elements facing Colonel Goodnight and his steers..."

With that, Wales could not read any further. His eyes glistened, and the words caught in his throat.

The painting was the last of hundreds his wife had painted. It was a depiction of Charles Goodnight leading a herd through Palo Duro Canyon in the 1800s. Abbie had taken the work to Vail in order to complete it at their Colorado home. She had not quite finished the painting when she became sick.

"She had finished everything except the foreman," Wales said. "This was actually Carl Smith's impression of Palo Duro Canyon. That artist, it's his rendition, and she copied the artist, but she got a little bleach in there and said that horse is not right. It's too big, and she made him smaller. No title, but it's longhorns entering the canyon-the first longhorns."

Wales softly closed the book. The paintings were more than colors, scenes, and portraits on paper. They were Abbie, and they spoke to Wales not only of her talent but also of who she was.

"I could spend a lot of time talking about the talent of Abbie," he said, "and how she was such a modest, unselfish person with her art."

He opened the book again, slowly looking at paintings on one page after another, each one telling a story, recalling a memory, speaking to him.

"There's her grandson...Look at that thing, golly...

"Oh, I get tears in my eyes looking at some of these...You see the humanness of her characters. Now who is this? I don't have any idea. But this is a different personality. And the expressions on the children are different."

Another page. Another pause. "Oh, isn't that dear?" he said.

Abbie dabbled in painting as a girl and in college, but her innate talent of making beauty out of a blank canvas blossomed under Ben Konis' instruction. She took classes with the Amarillo artist, increasing her skill and nurturing her lifelong love of the art. At one point, Konis told his class that Abbie was one of the finest local painters he had taught.

"Her instincts were so good," Wales said. "Instead of others being jealous, people that knew Abbie knew she was so gracious and so unassuming, anything but selfish."

Wales knew of her love for painting before they married. It went back to the days at UT. It was an outlet for her, an expression.

"I knew how she loved art," he said, "but she was so modest that the thought of someone wanting to look at her paintings was not in her makeup, which made the paintings even more treasured for those who knew Abbie."

As Wales talked, he turned a page and gazed. All of Abbie's paintings were treasures to him.

"Oh yeah, look at this. The bluebonnets on the hills. This is on the way to Austin. She had a feel especially for a person and a bush."

Abbie could paint wherever she could set up an easel, but most of her time was spent in her home studio, located in the attic above the kitchen.

"I would just kind of stay out of her way," he said. "The studio was nothing fancy, but it had a lot of space. Half of it was for supplies and storage. It had windows around two sides of the room facing the east and south. I would come home, and she would be painting."

As the pages brought Wales to paintings of their children and grandchildren, he reflected on that which was most precious to him.

"This is a flavor of what she liked to paint which helps people understand what she really enjoyed," he said. "This looks exactly like Wales and Tawney when they were that age...You can tell Wales is trying to pull her along but not hurt her."

The Maddens enjoyed traveling, and Abbie took her brushes, paints, and supplies with her, whether to Colorado or to Europe. Her paintings often reflected the scenes they had seen, the places they had been.

"She would paint in some kind of medium every time we'd stop and stay a couple of days," Wales said. "She would preserve her memory with her sketches and etchings. She just had that ability.

"Not many times with oils because they were too hard to travel with, yet she wouldn't miss a thing. If I'd go somewhere to fish, she would say, 'Let me stand on the bank.' She never fished, but she would watch me fish, and that was particularly fun in England because of the way they fished over there."

Wales estimated there were several hundred paintings in Abbie's collection, and her art hangs in the homes of friends, in the Madden offices on Polk Street and in Vail, and in their church, First Presbyterian.

"She never sold a one," Wales said. "I'd say, 'Oh, come on, take fifty dollars.' She'd say, 'Wales, I'm not going to sell any paintings.' I'd say, 'Can I sell a few?' 'No!'"

Abbie didn't become serious about her work until after she married. After decades of observing Abbie's work and watching her at work, Wales had an idea of what painting meant to her and why she never tired of the task, even to the end.

"Well, she probably didn't think it grandiose," he said, "but I think that she really could leave something that would mean a lot to a person, especially a person who had known her. She just could see beauty in nature. She just loved to paint."

The question couldn't help but be asked one last time: did Wales have a favorite one of his wife's paintings, although that may be like asking, "Who's your favorite child or grandchild?"

He opened the book again and turned to the page featuring the herd of longhorns heading into Palo Duro Canyon in the nineteenth century.

"The last one," Wales said. "The last one."

TALL TALES AND MARATHON
ROAD TRIPS

Wales Madden loves to spin a yarn. Occasionally, his yarns are true, but where's the fun in telling a tale if it isn't somewhat tall or, in many instances, a downright fib?

Wales has spent much of his life being a storyteller—partly prankster, partly yarn spinner. It's ingrained in his personality, a means of entertainment and levity to alleviate the seriousness of life.

"That's it," Wales said. "I don't recall ever planning a bull story. They just pop out. Why do they? Well, I have a big imagination. People enjoy the lack of seriousness in life. Most all of these stem from my instinct that says life is serious enough without making everything else serious."

There was no better place for story telling than on family road trips with the captive audience of his wife Abbie and their children, Wales III and Tawney. If a story entered his head, Wales was eager to tell it, using his dead-pan humor.

"He had a lot of opportunities to tell stories," Wales III said. "We always drove. In the fifties, sixties, even into the seventies, we rarely flew anywhere. It was always in a car, one of those good-looking station wagons.

1968 road trip

"But he told stories all the time. We didn't have video games, of course. So we played games, and he told stories. The older we got, we started figuring out they weren't true."

Even when they were young, Willie [Wales III] and Tawney probably knew that the tales of live volcanoes, giant eagles, and mountain ghosts they were listening to were in the same category as Paul Bunyan, but that didn't make them any less entertaining.

"The stories were right down their alley too," Wales said. "I don't know if they would have enjoyed all of those long road trips without my talking to them, but that helped boost them along, living with a fun sense of humor."

A gullible wife and mother was always present, too. Abbie had a tendency to believe that whatever was said was true-until she realized it wasn't. "Mom used to have a double-take," Willie said. "She did that for as long as I could remember, where it would dawn on her that something probably wasn't true. She would look away, and then right back."

Wales would test the gullibility of his young kids on trips to northern New Mexico. Did they know how Eagle Nest Lake was created? It was made by giant eagles who dug into the ground to make their nests.

"His stories always involved a fear factor," Willie said. "We were totally tormented growing up. His stories always pertained to kind of where we were."

Skiing trips that took them through northern New Mexico sometimes involved a story about Black Jack Ketchum, a notorious cowboy, train robber, and murderer living in the area in the late nineteenth century. Ketchum was hanged in Clayton, New Mexico, in 1901, Union County's only execution. When Ketchum dropped from the gallows, his weight caused his head to snap off, a particularly gruesome ending. That was a perfect scenario for Wales to embellish.

"His story usually involved the ghost of Black Jack Ketchum," Willie said.

"We would go off the highway," Wales recalled, "and we'd be on a remote road. I would say, 'Did you hear it? No, we're not far enough... Oh, wait, I think I saw his head! There it is!' And they would go wild screaming."

"The head coming off was true," Willie said. "He always wove in enough truth so that if you tried checking it out, you find out some of it did happen."

The dormant Capulin volcano near Raton, New Mexico, was too tempting a venue not to involve a story. There was usually a different version every time they drove the station wagon around the winding road that led to the top.

"It's a huge circle, and as you get up there, you can envision hot molten lava," Wales said. "The closer we got to the top, the more they were convinced they didn't want to go any more. It's a wonder the two of them have turned out as well as they have."

"Well, we spent a lot of time in therapy," Willie said.

However, none of Wales' stories were quite like the tales he told in, of all places, Washington, D.C., and Israel. There was a time when Wales' imagination and humor nearly landed him in hot water.

Wales was on business in Washington when he encountered a group of Saudis dressed in their traditional robes. He was alone, having a meal right next to them in the hotel's concierge lounge. The Saudis, Wales said, were in negotiations with the U.S. government to purchase some arms.

"I can remember engaging myself in their conversation," he said, "and asking if they needed any assistance in getting the government finally signed up so they could get back and buy some tanks.

"They didn't know what to think of me. Is this guy for real or not? When something like that happens, I can only go so far, and then I get a little frightened about what might happen."

Before Wales had finished his meal, a man in a business suit approached him and asked what he did exactly. Wales responded that he was with "the company."

"The man said, 'What is the company?' And I said, 'Well, there's just so much I can tell you. It will get all of us in trouble with the federal government if I tell you anymore,'" Wales said.

The next morning, about 6:00 a.m., there was a firm knock on the door of Wales' hotel room. It was the same man, but this time he was in uniform. He was a two-star general.

"He was in charge of that group from Saudi Arabia, and he wanted to talk to me," Wales said. "I said, 'Sir, sir, I was a Seaman, First Class, World War II, sir. I was just joking!"

Thus ended Wales' short-lived career as a CIA operative, but it didn't end his practical jokes at the expense of Middle Easterners.

Back in the 1970s, Texas Governor Dolph Briscoe selected about a dozen men from across the state to go to Israel at their own expense. It was a five-day tour of the country to familiarize themselves with the issues Israel faced and to become allies in helping the country gain aid from the United States.

"The purpose was very legitimate," he said, "but also pretty boring." Alas, when things became boring, Wales' mind often kicked into high gear.

The group traveled from Jerusalem to Tel Aviv. One day was devoted to agriculture, cattle in particular. Wales thought he would mix cattle with camels, an animal a country like Israel is noted for.

"I said to a group of people that one of the things I was personally undertaking was the fact we have a very large ranch in Texas, and we can't really control and patrol the herds of cattle, and I have an idea of how we can use camels," Wales said.

Yes, Mr. Madden, they politely replied. Tell us about this idea.

"The first thing we have to do is design a saddle that would have a pull-up like a window shade on the stirrup. You pull it down, put your foot in the stirrup, and it would shoot you up, and put you on top of the camel," Wales told the incredulous hosts. "Then you are equal-the camel and the cattle."

The Israelis asked if this kind of mount was dangerous. Wales said it involved a bit of trial and error.

"I told them the first couple of times, they just tossed me over the other side of the camel, but it didn't hurt," he said.

Wales must have had an honest face to sell a camel story full of bull. The next night the mayor of Tel Aviv picked up Wales to take him to a reception which was attended by many of the top Israeli government officials. At one point during the evening, a group was huddled around a man who had heard Wales' cock-and-bull/camel story the previous day.

"And I can hear this guy saying, '...and the stirrup, you pull it down, and you put your foot in, and you have to be careful because it will really throw you...'" Wales said. "I wanted to say, 'Hey, I was just joking.' How do you stop that situation? I didn't want to say, 'Hey, I was lying all the time.' I just let it go. Life is full of funny things if you see it from the right perspective."

Those incidents happened when Wales was traveling solo, but if a trip didn't include business, Abbie and the children were with him. For Willie and Tawney traveling as a family was a huge part of growing up and had an impact on their lives.

"Traveling together was important because, subliminally, I knew that some day they would have families, and that kind of bonding with your family was part of the whole process," Wales said.

There were yearly treks to certain destinations. In the fall, there were trips to Austin for Longhorn football games, often more than once. En route, Wales put his kids through Texas Football 101.

"You had to memorize the roster, or at least the first and second teams, and there would be a test before we got to Austin," Willie said.

In the winter, there were ski trips to northern New Mexico, to places like Sipapu, or to Vail and Winter Park in Colorado. Frequently they would caravan with family friends who had children roughly the same ages as Willie and Tawney. There was one European ski vacation to Austria and Switzerland. No caravan on that one.

1972 Kitzbuhel, Austria

"I was never a really good skier. I would stay away from what would be a dangerous slope for me, but I could ski the slopes I wanted to ski," Wales said. "I took lessons and felt very comfortable."

Willie and Tawney were advanced and competitive, rarely encountering a slope they wouldn't attack. About Abbie on the slopes Wales said, "She was good, but very, very cautious."

"Normally, if we were going for three days, there would be a day that was a lesson," Willie said. "We spent a lot of time at ski school, which was good. As we got older, the private lessons were less about teaching and more about cutting lines so you could get more runs in."

1970 Vail, CO

But no trips were as memorable as the annual drives to California and Disneyland. Beginning in the early 1960s, there might have been as many as a dozen trips to the famed amusement park which had been open only six or seven years.

The trip usually lasted about two weeks with the Maddens first arriving in San Diego to spend several days at the Hotel del Coronado, the iconic beach resort hotel. The California trip was a summer tradition, as were trips to their 3 Forks Ranch in Colorado.

Disneyland became a hand-me-down trip for the children of Willie and Tawney. Despite the numerous times through the gates, it has never become routine.

"It's still not old," Willie said. "We've been trying to figure out when we can go by ourselves and not take anyone with us. When you're little-I don't want to say it's magical—but technology even back in the sixties was unbelievable. We got to see it change and evolve and become a lot more high-tech."

On several trips to California the Maddens visited Lloyd Hand, Wales' old buddy from his UT days. Hand, who had been involved with Lyndon Johnson in his political campaigns, was now involved in the movie industry, which was just fine with the Maddens.

"He would always have three or four international stars at a party he would give for us," Wales said.

On one occasion Hand arranged for the Maddens to be on the lot to see filming of the sit-com *McHale's Navy* with Ernest Borgnine and Tim Conway, as well as the sit-com *The Munsters*.

"We didn't go to the Hands' every summer, but frequently, and they always had some function going on," Willie said. "I remember seeing Natalie Wood there. Steve McQueen was at one of them, and a lot of them I knew were movie stars, but I didn't have a clue who they were."

1964 L to R: Sen. Birch Bayh, TM, Vic Damon, Chip Hand, Natalie Wood, Steve McQueen, Lucy Johnson, Kathy & Bridget Hand, WM3

There were special trips as well. Wales was not one to miss opportunities, making sure they went to the Seattle and New York World Fairs.

"It seemed like I got lost at one of them," Willie said.

"Oh, you got lost at more than one," Wales said. "Your mother was just panicking."

Being in the car for hours and hours and miles and miles was a lesson in itself. They needed to create their own entertainment which resulted in some of Wales' stories, and because familiarity bred contempt, ground rules were needed also.

They played games such as finding different cars, three each of eight categories, or guessing how many different states' license plates could be seen in one day.

"You had to do something for the twelve hours you were in the car," Willie said.

Wales instituted the three-warning rule. The third warning for misbehavior meant no swimming at the motel pool that night. Rest assured, both Tawney and Willie pushed it to at least two warnings every day.

On one particular trip, however, none of that was needed. It was one of the few plane trips they took as a family. They went to South America for an eventful, educational trip which included the countries of Ecuador, Panama, Peru, Chile, Argentina, and Brazil.

"The thing I remember about that trip was people eating guinea pigs," Willie said. "They would grill them on the street and eat them right there."

Wales nodded. That one was no tall tale.

Additional Photos

1967 Hawaii

3 FORKS AND A CANYON

In Colorado, near the Wyoming border, forty miles north of Steamboat Springs, there is a little slice of heaven located at the confluence of the South Fork, North Fork, and Middle Fork of the Little Snake River. Appropriately called the 3 Forks Ranch, it comprises 4,000 deeded acres and 25,000 service lease acres with the river flowing right through the middle of the deeded land. 3 Forks served as a Madden family retreat for about fifteen years.

In 1963, Wales went in with two other parties to purchase the ranch. Wales and Abbie's mother, Jesse Cowden Tamney, each owned a twenty-five percent share. The remaining fifty percent was owned by Murl Hayter.

3 Forks was primarily a summertime retreat. The family enjoyed trout fishing, hiking, and horseback riding for ten days to two weeks each summer. Usually when the Maddens went to 3 Forks, the children's grandmother Jesse and her second husband Ben were there as well, having traveled from their home in Midland.

1970 SM, WM3, Abbie

1970 SM, Ben, Jessie, WM3 and WM

"Oh, Abbie's mother loved it too," Wales said.

The accommodations, which were not luxurious but simply practical, included a guest house, some bunkhouses, and a foreman's house. The guest house kitchen was small, but the dining room could seat twelve to fourteen people. Downstairs there were two bedrooms and two bathrooms, and upstairs there were two bedrooms with bunk beds.

"There would be times," Willie said, "when there would be ten people for two bedrooms."

1971 3 Forks headquarters

3 Forks wasn't easily accessible with the last forty-five miles being dirt roads. The fishing, the air, the beauty, simply the escape, justified any difficulty encountered en route.

1968 Camper and horse trailer trip

"We got the jeep stuck every summer," Willie said. "We used to take these jeep trails. The house was less than a half mile from the forest service, so they had these jeep trails all over. We'd get out and drive around, and pretty soon, we'd be sliding down the hill sideways until we hit an aspen. We did that several times."

For Wales, it simply gave him a chance to be with his children and grandchildren in his beloved outdoors.

"I loved to trout fish," Wales said, "and I never got tired of it. Abbie loved it in the same way," Wales said. "I was kind of an outdoor guy. I didn't want to wear anything but Levis."

1966 fishing   *1970 still fishing*

The Maddens had an agreement with the Hayter family allowing the Hayters to run cattle and sheep on the land as long as they maintained fences and irrigation ditches.

"The Hayters got tired of it," Willie said, "because it was an expensive cattle operation. The irrigation ditches would wash out every winter. The elk would tear the fences down, so it was a high-maintenance cattle business. If I remember right, they came to us and said it's just too expensive to run cattle."

3 Forks was sold to a Chicago businessman who eventually sold it to the current ownership group. Today, it is a high-end luxury retreat for fly fishing, hunting, and downhill skiing. It offers world-class dining and all other amenities. One night in a master suite costs $845 per person. Askmen.com listed 3 Forks' luxury lodges among the top ten in the country. It is now a far cry from its days of ten people sharing two bedrooms.

1967   *1970 Riding an irrigation ditch*

The memories of 3 Forks have remained with Wales, but an outdoor site much closer to home has resonated as well. Palo Duro Canyon, south of Amarillo, has long been a favorite place for Wales. Within the canyon there is a famous venue that he helped to create.

For more than fifty years, the Palo Duro Canyon Pioneer Amphitheater, a unique outdoor theater carved into the base of the canyon, has been home to the musical *Texas!* In the early 1960s, the theater and the play grew out of the dreams and hard work of a group of people which included Wales.

"I want very much to give credit to the husband and wife at West Texas State on this," Wales said. "She was a very exasperating, yet inspiring lady. She spotted me as someone who wanted to do something creative in Palo Duro Canyon. They deserve much of the credit for that. I don't."

Wales was referring to WT professor Ples Harper and his wife, Margaret. Ples was head of the modern language department, and Margaret was the driving force for the creation of a musical unique to the Panhandle, if only there were somewhere in the canyon for the production.

Margaret read an article in *Reader's Digest* about Paul Green, a playwright and author in North Carolina. Green had penned several outdoor dramas across the country. In 1960, Margaret and William A. Moore, chairman of the WT speech department, invited Green to

Amarillo and Canyon to see whether he would write a musical about the Texas Panhandle.

As Margaret reached out to friends and colleagues in Canyon, interest in the prospect of an outdoor theater began to grow. Soon a small group of Canyon families funded Green's trip to Texas. According to those in attendance at that first meeting in 1961, Green immediately dedicated himself to the project of bringing the history of the High Plains to the stage.

In May 1961 at the Randall County Courthouse, the Texas Panhandle Heritage Foundation was established. Margaret Harper, as president, led a seven-member board of directors. Support was widespread. Eventually, forty west Texas counties were represented, and the foundation was incorporated in September 1961.

The foundation's primary goal was the construction of an amphitheater, its back drop formed by a cliff six hundred feet high. The idea of a similar structure was first introduced in the 1930s when Guy Carlander, an Amarillo architect, drew up elaborate plans at the suggestion of WT President Joseph Hill. Being made during the Depression, those plans never came to fruition. Some thirty years later, the idea was revived.

The project needed funding, and the foundation knew whom to approach for fundraising. Two committees were launched, one chaired by Lawrence Hagy and Mary Miles Batson, the other chaired by Wales. The Amarillo Area Foundation agreed to supervise the collection and expenditure of the funds.

Wales used his power of persuasion and his network of influential friends to begin raising money. One of his first calls was to Pete and Wanda Gilvin, whose ranch home was perched on the canyon's rim.

Governor Visits Scene of Drama

Gov. Price Daniel, left, and Wales Madden Jr this morning visited the site of the proposed symphonic drama which will be produced in Palo Duro Canyon State Park. The governor said the drama would aid in bringing tourists to the area. Madden is chairman of the campaign for drama capital funds.

Governor Price Daniel and WM
Source: Amarillo Globe-News

"Pete was the leader of anything we did at the canyon," Wales said, "and a key supporter of building the amphitheater. They both loved that canyon. These weren't his exact words, but Pete said if I could take the lead in getting ideas like where the theater would be located and who would run it, then he would furnish a large part of the funding."

The money was raised, and construction began after permission to build the 1,600-seat Pioneer Amphitheater was secured from the State Parks Board.

"He [Ples Harper] wanted to establish something in the canyon that memorialized the things he loved about the canyon," Wales said. "I had that same goal, but I knew more about people and how to get them interested. It wasn't that difficult to sell the idea."

The Amarillo Symphony performed the first production at the amphitheater in 1965. Between June 17 and September 6, 1965, the foundation staged a sound and light show, *Thundering Sounds of the West*, which attracted 36,000 visitors.

That success indicated what could be possible. With the backing of WT, Paul Green's famous musical drama *Texas!* opened the following year. In fifty years more than 2.5 million people have made their way to the outdoor theater.

For Wales, the musical drama and the amphitheater were the lure to get the public inside his beloved Palo Duro Canyon, an experience most of them would not have had otherwise.

"When you had the stage, people wanted to come down," he said. "I'd say sixty percent of them had never been in the canyon. Word gets around. It was an excuse to get people out of the city and to come down. It has such a good reputation now, and how wonderful that is."

Wales is insistent on giving a huge part of the credit to the Harpers. He's just glad to have played a part in helping put a gem at the bottom of the canyon that has been so dear to him for decades.

WALES & WILLIE: IN BUSINESS TOGETHER

This much seemed certain for Wales Madden III: it's a lot more fun and satisfying to work *with* his dad than *for* him. During high school and between semesters at the University of Texas, Wales III found himself at the ranch near Clayton, New Mexico, working during the hot summers and breaking ice on leased wheat pastures during the winters.

"I made fourteen dollars a day plus three meals, and I slept in a sleeping bag at an old Catholic Church in Moses, New Mexico," he said. "I thought I could make more money rolling coins at the bank (in Amarillo), and *it* was air-conditioned."

But it would soon get better for young Willie-oh, not that summer, but in due time. Following his mom and dad's footsteps, he graduated from UT in 1977 with a degree in Finance and earned his MBA from the university two years later.

After graduation Willie watched as fellow classmates interviewed with banks and with investment firms like Goldman Sachs, but his path had already been mapped out. Father and son went into business together in 1979, the year Willie graduated with his MBA. It was never really planned or discussed. That was just the way it played out over time.

"He grew up familiar with what I was doing," Wales said of his son, "and I encouraged him to take over."

Wales, of course, had spent more than twenty-five years working as an attorney, first for Shamrock and later helping Mesa Petroleum chairman and high school friend Boone Pickens in the expansion Mesa's oil and gas exploration.

Wales often left his son to run the business as he had more pressing commitments. That alone showed the confidence Wales placed in Willie who was only twenty-four.

Wales and Mike Myers, were co-chairmen of the 1980 John Connally presidential campaign. The former Texas governor was a long-time friend of Wales.

With campaign offices in Washington and Houston, many of the trips for the campaign were made in the Madden's Cessna 210. Wales was the pilot if the weather was clear, but if the weather wouldn't cooperate, Willie took over. Wales didn't spend much time in Amarillo and had little focus on business during that hectic period.

Cessna 210 owned by Pat Oles, Walter Kellogg and WM

It was then that the Maddens bought their first computers, and Wales and Willie became involved in one of their first deals together, a purchasing group led by J.W. Smith, chairman of United National Bank in Dallas, and his sons, Scott and Steve. The group bought banks in Denison and Sherman, holding them until they were sold in the late 1980s.

"I went from being in school to being on the board of two banks," Willie said.

The Maddens' major investments, however, were and continue to be in a main staple of this region. For about fifteen years, from around 1970 into the early 1980s, Wales, and later Willie, were in the cattle business, along with Pat and Chuck Babb, Jim Austin, Glen Parkey, and George Morris.

Most of the cattle were pastured on the family ranch near Clayton, where Willie had learned about the sweat and calluses of the cattle business. At its height, with over 4,000 cattle in inventory, their operation encompassed leased ranches and wheat pasture in northeastern New Mexico and in Texas, cattle in feedlots near Pecos and in the Texas Panhandle, and importing, or "crossing," Mexican steers into Texas and New Mexico. By the mid-eighties, however, that had all come to an end.

"We decided to get out," Willie said, "because of the capital requirements necessary to be trading cattle on a weekly basis and the inherent risks associated with the ag business. Some years were good, and some years stunk. You can't control the market or the weather, so it was tough for us to make money consistently."

The Clayton ranch was sold in the early 1980s to Allen and Robert Durrett, the nephews of Wales' old friend Eldon Durrett.

In 1984 the Maddens reconnected with Jim Southern, an Amarillo native, who had worked for George Morris selling life insurance for the Prudential Insurance Company. Wales, Willie, George, and Jim shared an office on Ninth Street until Jim decided to enter the Harvard Graduate School of Business. After completing his MBA, Jim went to work for the Maddens. Together they formed one of the earliest "search" companies, Nova Capital.

Nova and its key financial partners, Paul Ferri of Matrix Partners and H. Irving (Irv) Grousbeck, soon bought Uniform Printing, a division of a public company, that specialized in printing insurance endorsement forms. Uniform Printing, at the time, had five production facilities and fifteen distribution warehouses spread across the U.S. After a few tough years that involved union battles, consolidating operations, and unusual personal matters, the business flourished. The board of directors—Southern, Ferri, Grousbeck, Wales, and Willie—approved several stock buybacks during that time, finally selling the business in the early nineties. Uniform Printing remains one of the best investments the Maddens have ever made. Additionally, the concept and funding mechanism behind Nova Capital and the purchase of Uniform Printing became a case study in a textbook written by Grousbeck for graduate business students at Stanford University.

In 1996, the Maddens reorganized and consolidated their family businesses into a single entity, Gore Creek Capital, Ltd., named after the creek that runs through Vail, Colorado, their home-away-from-home. Today, Gore Creek has investments in oil and gas, public and private equities, and in real estate with son-in-law Dean Macfarlan, Tawney's husband.

Wales terms the business a "family deal." Even as he approaches his eighty-ninth birthday, he goes to Suite 501 in the Amarillo Building at 301 N. Polk Street almost every day.

"It's fun when things work right," Willie said. "It's nice because dad has seen all the rodeos before. People call them 'mentors'-and I'm not sure that's the right word-but he's always there. Nothing surprises or shakes him. He gets mad occasionally, but never at me. It's just good to have that wisdom and experience."

Family businesses have been known to strain relationships, but that's not been the case for the Maddens. "It never has been an issue," Wales said. "We love and respect each other. We don't always agree on what to do, but it seems like when that happens, we reach a point and say, 'OK, let's do this,' and we move on."

"He gives me a lot of rope," Willie said. "Now if I can just keep him from opening the mail."

Wales and Willie agree that the most indispensable person at Gore Creek is Ann Payne. To call her a secretary would be a gross understatement. She is an administrative assistant, organizer, scheduler, simplifier, often the glue that keeps the daily work together. Ann has worked for Wales for twenty-eight years, but he knew her earlier, when she worked for Gene Edwards at the First National Bank. He would see her when he went to the bank for personal business or for a board meeting.

Ann left the bank and went to work for George Morris when he and Wales shared an office on Ninth Street. When George passed away in the late eighties, Ann went to work for Joe Morris, George's nephew, and for the Maddens.

Eventually, when the building on Ninth was sold, Wales moved to the Fisk Building, which is now the Marriott Courtyard Hotel. Later he moved to the Amarillo Building. Each step of the way, Ann went with him.

"She is totally honest and very smart," Wales said. "She's a very bright person. I don't want to think what it would be like without her."

"When she came, she started doing what we had others do, but she picked up the slack and was doing things that had not been done before," Willie said. "There's not very many we trust to the degree we trust Ann. If she decided not to go to work here anymore, it would take at least two people to replace her."

As for Wales and Willie-which sounds a bit like a country singing act-this father and son have made music together in the business world for nearly forty years. And it has worked.

"Ours is a rare relationship that's been built over the years on affection and trust," Wales said.

AFTER ABBIE

Wales and his family were confronted with a sudden change in 2003, the kind of occurrence one never expects, although it can happen to anyone at any time. The news of it takes the breath away from a spouse, filling him with worry and anxiety.

Abbie Madden's medical report was grim: adenocarcinoma, often called smoker's cancer. Making the diagnosis even more difficult to accept was the fact that she had never been a smoker.

Abbie went to M.D. Anderson in Houston for treatment. There was a shadow on the upper lobe of her left lung. A biopsy confirmed the mass was cancerous. During surgery to remove the upper lobe, biopsies were performed on the nodules which had been found on the exterior of the lower lung. They proved to be lung cancer as well, meaning the disease had metastasized. Abbie's cancer was stage four.

"One of the doctors told me, 'I'm afraid she's not going to live,'" Wales said. "The other doctor said, 'I promise you, you don't need to fear about her death anytime soon.'"

"Mom's oncologist told us he thought the cancer would be slow growing," Willie said, "and that probably something else would get her before the lung cancer would."

Abbie and Wales returned to Amarillo and took it one precious day at a time. One day led to a week, to a month, to a year, and another year, and another. This regal and charming woman may not have looked very tough, but she was a fierce fighter.

The cancer was dormant-no chemo or radiation. Between trips to Houston for tests, she threw herself into her painting and being the same loving companion to her husband as she had been for more than fifty years. Knowing the unwanted cancer might return, they were just grateful for each sunrise and sunset.

Then, nine years later, in early 2012, Abbie started feeling some pain. Tests revealed eighteen suspicious spots, including several in her bones and hips. The cancer had returned, and radiation therapy was begun on her hips.

Abbie was also treated with an experimental protein inhibitor, a genetically targeted drug. Most patients who had taken that drug and had had good responses were in their fifties, not Abbie's age of eighty-one. She may have been one of the oldest patients ever to take the experimental drug.

"At the end of the day, I think the protein inhibitor put her in a tailspin," Willie said.

Alma Faye Madden died on August 26, 2012, at the age of eighty-two. She and Wales had been married just two months shy of sixty years. In the ensuing weeks and months, Wales found himself not really living but merely existing in a haze of grief and loss.

"I don't know if I was ever comfortable about, 'Don't feel bad, you'll be with her in the hereafter,'" Wales said. "I was just going along, going to church, working, trying to go up to Colorado when I could."

The family's grief in their loss was greatly tempered by their assurance of Abbie's salvation in Christ. The family could see that Abbie's death affected their father not only emotionally but also mentally.

"I wasn't worried about mom, and we're still not. It's hard for any of us to grieve about her standing on streets of gold and looking at the very face of Almighty God. It's sad because she's gone and we all miss her, but for her, it's great. Tawney and all of us have coped with this because, with a high degree of certainty, we know where she is, and we know there will be a great reunion someday. But Dad is different. He was older when this happened. There was a time when mentally and emotionally it was not good," Willie said.

Thankfully, others besides family could see that Wales was hurting. Directed by God's healing hand, Virginia Maynard saw his pain.

Wales and Virginia first knew each other back at Amarillo High in the 1940s, but nearly seventy years later, they were to become better acquainted. In late 2012 Virginia understood what Wales was facing. She had faced the same loneliness and sadness when John, her husband of nearly sixty-one years, died in March of that same year.

With the death of a husband or wife, the partner loses more than a love. They lose a part of themselves as well. The days aren't quite as bright, the nights are longer and colder, and the world just looks different, no matter how strong the resolve is to carry on.

A few months after Abbie's passing, Virginia saw her old friend walking against the wind into United Market Street. He was downcast and looked defeated. As she recalls, Wales was barely putting one foot in front of the other.

"It never even occurred to me that it was a male-female thing," Virginia said. "I thought, 'Here's my good friend. I know how he feels.' I called Wales and said to meet me for lunch at Red Lobster. I thought Red Lobster sounded like a good non-seductive spot. That was the last thing I had in mind. Also, a friend of mine at church said, 'Virginia, you must do something about Wales. You need to help him snap out of it.' He wasn't snapping."

Wales thought he had been coming out of church, not going into the grocery store, but he defers to Virginia. Nevertheless, they met for lunch at Red Lobster and split the check. It was a meeting that set them on a path that would enrich both of their lives in ways they never thought possible, the culmination of a meandering journey of parallel lives that led them to each other.

Virginia Irwin graduated from Amarillo High in 1947. She was a cheerleader and a class favorite for two years, popular in her own way.

After high school, Virginia attended Cottey College for Women in Nevada, Missouri, transferring to the University of Texas her sophomore year. She and Abbie were in the same Kappa Kappa Gamma pledge class, and they both lived on the third floor of the Kappa house.

"We were just kind of thrown together," Virginia said. "She was pretty and always busy. Abbie was not among my closest friends at the time, but I admired her. She came from money, but she was so unpretentious, so natural."

After they pledged the sorority, Virginia remembers Abbie's father sending her a huge Cadillac in the Kappa Kappa Gamma colors of blue on blue.

"We all stood there with our mouths open," she said, "and Abbie was like, 'Oh, no!' She was kind of embarrassed he would do such a thing."

Virginia crossed paths with Wales at UT more than she had at Amarillo High. He and a large group of his friends from Amarillo were Phi Delts, thanks to Wales. She said those hometown guys would come to her rescue if needed, but truth be told, she was more interested in the guys in the Sigma Alpha Epsilon and Kappa Sigma fraternities.

"I always knew what Wales was doing because of Abbie," she said.

Not everyone from Amarillo had a car in those days. If word spread that someone was driving home, his trip usually became a car pool north for a weekend. "If we heard that Wales was driving home at a certain time from Austin to Amarillo, he would fill up the car, and I remember a couple of times being in on that ride," Virginia said.

"There weren't many conditions," Wales said, "but one was there would be only one restroom stop on the trip."

Virginia met her future husband John Maynard in a Spanish class in junior high, and they were well enough acquainted in high school that Virginia knew who he was. Their interest in one another blossomed during Virginia's first year at UT. Unfortunately for her, John was in school at Stanford University in Palo Alto, California.

"At the time, Virginia was a budding close friend, and John and I were very good friends," Wales said. "But she was outstandingly cute."

John Maynard and Virginia Irwin were married on June 23, 1951, in Amarillo, just a few weeks after both had graduated from college and one year before Wales and Abbie were married.

John and Virginia lived on Puget Sound for two years while John was in the Navy. When John was discharged from the Navy in 1953, they returned to Amarillo to make their home. Making their way into the Panhandle from the west was a homecoming.

"Once we got to about Adrian, I thought this was the most beautiful country in the world," Virginia said.

John began working for his father at John Maynard Lumber Company where he had started doing odd jobs as a boy. The company grew into Maywood, which at its peak had more than 500 employees. John and Virginia had four children-Kathryn, Johnny, Tom and Martha. They produced seven grandchildren and seven great-grandchildren.

During the late 1950s and into the 1960s, after returning from the service, young married couples settled in with their children and spent their spare time together. The Madden and Maynard families made numerous ski trips together to New Mexico and Colorado. When the Morris and Babb families joined them, there would be a caravan of station wagons traveling the mountain roads.

"Those were such fun, treasured years," Virginia said. "It was such a special time, but we didn't realize how special when it was happening."

John died in March 2012, a few months shy of their sixty-first anniversary. He had battled Alzheimer's disease for several years, although he did not suffer a personality change. It was actually a heart attack that claimed John's life.

"I would walk through the room in that last year, and he would say, 'There's my beautiful wife of sixty years with many more to come,'" Virginia said.

It was five months later in August 2012 that Abbie Madden died. Two old friends who had lost their mates of sixty years were each now adrift, in need of an anchor. They began acquiring that anchor when they shared salmon and a salad at Red Lobster.

"I knew so well how he felt, and I knew his heart was aching because mine was too," Virginia said. "Periodically, one of us would tear up, and when one would tear up, the other would too."

They began to meet regularly for lunch, usually after church but sometimes during the week. Wales could tell this was leading to more than just mealtime company and, as he said, "She was not discouraging."

"I remember one of our early dates when Wales said that he was not interested in matrimony," Virginia said, "and I thought, 'Oh my gosh, that's the strangest thing I ever heard!'"

Wales said it was not out of the ordinary for the two of them to fall in love. Their needs were the same. There was the similarity of their spouses, and they had similar families.

"So to fall in love, gosh, yes," Wales said. "I was taken by her the first time we had lunch. But I also had the advantage of knowing her and John, seeing her in church. We had so much to talk about."

They agreed from the outset not to marry. They didn't feel it was necessary, and it might even complicate things that didn't need complicating. They are comfortable in their own homes, and they see each other almost every day. Remaining unmarried has not diminished their love for each other.

"Virginia has helped me continue a normal life, almost," Wales said. "Without Virginia, I would still be going to the office, going home, working out at the gym, and that's all. We go together so much. Being able to have her talk to and to go with, I'm very lucky."

"Wales is a wonderful pal, friend, wonderful person," Virginia said. "I've always valued him as someone I look up to. He's just fun to be with. We have a good time. He's good company and kind of an incentive for the day."

"I do have lots of activities and interests, fortunately, but I look forward to seeing him usually at the end of the day. I know somehow we'll see each other. I've said this before, that we don't have very many days left so we ought to see each other about every day. I'm really conscious of missing him if I don't see him at the end of the day."

They found each other at a time when they both needed a companion, a partner, someone to laugh with, to share a sunset, to reminisce, to look forward to the next morning. They saw many of the strengths of their longtime spouses in one another.

Large holes in their hearts have been stitched, and their hearts have grown to make room for each of them to add the other to the lifetime love they had for Abbie Madden and John Maynard.

A consistent and deep relationship with the Lord has been steadfast within Wales even as he approaches the age of ninety years, and his health is not what it once was. After Abbie's death he has shared that love of Christ with Virginia as they share their love for each other.

"Faith is still in my picture," he said. "My health is not superb. To some extent I feel frightened, though 'frightened' is often an overly weighted word. Virginia and I have talked about this before, but what we want is to be able to be in love with each other. Whichever one goes first, the other will probably follow right along.

"I don't have less faith, but maybe a feeling of having less time to devote to it. When you are in a situation where you have a reasonable and justifiable concern of your health at eighty-nine, come on, how long do you think your health is going to last? Virginia and I have talked about this so much. She and I each share the love the other has in Christ, and there's no shame in that."

Wales and Virginia—a love late in life, at just the right time.

IT'S A WONDERFUL LIFE

When reflecting on Wales Madden, Jr., a fellow by the name of George Bailey comes to mind. Bailey? George Bailey? Was he a classmate at Amarillo High? A Phi Delt at Texas? Maybe he served with him in the Navy, or did Wales help run one of his political campaigns?

No, no to all of them. Actually George Bailey doesn't really exist-except in a black and white film around Christmas time. Jimmy Stewart brought the character to the screen in *It's A Wonderful Life*, the timeless classic released in 1946, about the same time that Wales was discharged from the Navy.

Bailey followed in his father's footsteps in the same profession-banking. He was a civic leader, promoter, and supporter to his hometown Bedford Falls. He was a family man with a wife and two children.

Likewise, Wales followed in his father's footsteps in the same profession-law. He was a civic leader, promoter, and supporter of his hometown Amarillo. He is a family man with a wife and two children.

Bailey's life was thrown into chaos, and for awhile, he became despondent. Wales' life has never been chaotic, but he has known heartache and disappointment, the difficult valleys that a long life will bring. Like George Bailey, Wales carved a life from helping others without asking for much, if anything, in return. The reward of changing and improving lives, careers and causes was more than enough.

"My life has been blessed by the Lord. If you can say that, what else is there to say?" Wales said. "I do think I've tried to help those less fortunate, and that certainly includes setting an example for a relationship with Christ."

The list of the institutions, the organizations, and the people Wales has helped through advice, service, insight, and financial aid is long–likely longer than any other in Amarillo. From his alma mater, the University of Texas, to his hometown and his church, Wales has given more than sixty-five years of unselfish volunteerism because that's the way he wanted it.

"Dad likes jobs that don't pay," joked his son Willie. "His primary focus when you look back is education and furthering the cause of education. It's not with an elitist mentality, but really more of a common man approach.

"When Dad takes on a project or commits to serve on a board, then you get 100 percent of him. Not everybody does that."

The beginning of this life is marked, September 1, 1927. Now, in the clear twilight of his life, the other final date will come, as it comes for everyone. But it's what connects those dates that paints life's pictures. It's the dash connecting date of birth to date of death. That symbol, the long line of dashes, can play out for years, decades, into different centuries. What did we do with that dash? Did we make a difference; did we shine a light for others; did we do what the Lord commanded?

To live and love. In Wales' downtown Amarillo office are many pictures of him with presidents and other dignitaries, of famous coaches and educators, and of family, of children and grandchildren, of his late wife Abbie. They speak of life and love, of a rich life in the dash.

In the movie's climax, George Bailey runs home to a house full of people, men and women in that fictional community who were helped by him through the years who have in turn come to help him.

Looking at Wales Madden as a reflection of George Bailey, imagine the crowd. Imagine the young and old, the black, brown and white, from all walks and from all places, who could fill up a large house or even a city block, who could rise up and say, "Thank you for your service; thank you for making a difference!"

For Wales Madden, Jr., it has been—and continues to be—a wonderful life.

October 2016

AFTERWORD

The family met in Dallas to celebrate Wales' eighty-ninth birthday over Labor Day weekend in 2016. Wales was surrounded by children, grandchildren and great grandchildren. In the midst of that confusion, a quiet gathered around Wales. Dean Macfarlan, Wales' favorite (and only) son-in-law read a passage from the Old Testament that fits his father-in-law, Jeremiah 9: 23-24:

> "This is what the Lord says: Don't let the wise boast in their wisdom, or the powerful boast in their power, or the rich boast in their riches.

> "But those who wish to boast should boast in this alone: that they truly know me and understand that I am the Lord who demonstrates unfailing love and who brings justice and righteousness to the earth, and that I delight in these things. I, the Lord, have spoken!"

ABOUT THE AUTHOR

Jon Mark Beilue, like Wales Madden, grew up in the Texas Panhandle, although it was some 30 years later and in a much smaller place. Beilue grew up in the small town of Groom, the son of a farmer and a high school English and journalism teacher.

In high school, after summers and weekends toiling on the farm, he didn't know what he wanted to do with his life but he knew it should involve air-conditioning. Working on the school paper gave him an idea.

Beilue went to Texas Tech, worked on the *University Daily* student newspaper, and graduated with a B.A. in journalism in 1981. He was hired first as a sportswriter with the *Amarillo Globe-News* that summer.

Thinking he would be there a couple of years, it has been more than 35. The first 25 years were in the sports department, the last 17 of them as sports editor. In 2006, he became the Globe-News' general columnist, the first for the newspaper since the 1970s.

He has won numerous statewide and national awards in his career, and a book of his columns, *This Might Be A Good Story,* was published in 2014.

Jon Mark and his wife Sandy have two grown sons.

Printed in the United States
By Bookmasters